PENGUIN

A VIEW FROM THE BENCH

Judge Joseph Wapner was born in Los Angeles, and attended the University of Southern California. He became a California municipal court judge in 1959, and two years later was elevated to the Los Angeles County Superior Court, where he remained until his retirement in 1979. He began "The People's Court" in 1981.

JUDGE JOSEPH

A. WAPNER

A VIEW FROM THE BENCH

Penguin Books

PENGUIN BOOKS
Published by the Penguin Group
Viking Penguin Inc., 40 West 23rd Street,
New York, New York 10010, U.S.A.
Penguin Books Ltd, 27 Wrights Lane,
London W8 5TZ, England
Penguin Books Australia Ltd, Ringwood,
Victoria, Australia
Penguin Books Canada Ltd, 2801 John Street,
Markham, Ontario, Canada L3R 1B4
Penguin Books (N.Z.) Ltd, 182–190 Wairau Road,
Auckland 10, New Zealand

Penguin Books Ltd, Registered Offices:
Harmondsworth, Middlesex, England

First published in the United States of America by
Simon & Schuster, Inc. 1987
Published in Penguin Books 1988

3 5 7 9 10 8 6 4 2

LIBRARY OF CONGRESS CATALOGING IN PUBLICATION DATA
Wapner, Joseph A.
A view from the bench.
Originally published: New York: Simon and
Schuster, c1987.
1. Judicial opinions—California.   2. Wapner,
Joseph A.   3. Justice, Administration of—California.
I. Title.
[KF213.W33W36 1988]   347.73   88-9916
ISBN 0-451-82193-9   347.307

Printed in the United States of America by
Krueger-Ringier, Inc., Dresden, Tennessee
Set in Times Roman

For Mickey

ACKNOWLEDGMENTS

ANY EFFORT AT RECOLLECTION of a life in the law is inevitably a communal effort. Cases blend together, fade in and out, lose and gather focus. Their lessons remain long after their facts. To recall the cases involved in this history took the kind cooperation of many fine lawyers and lay people who had worked with me on the bench and before me as trial lawyers.

In particular, I thank my colleagues Justice James Hastings, Judge Christopher Markey, Judge Ralph Nutter, Justice Armand Arabian, Gordon Wright, Art Manella, Joseph Ball, Paul Geragos, Marvin Part, Robert Courtney, Richard Tarlow, Irving Axelrad, and Stan Zipzer. If I have omitted anyone, I apologize. Without the help of these kind people, this volume could not be.

In my life on the bench, non-lawyers were also invaluable in helping me ransack the past for the lessons of today. Most especially, I thank my former and long-time clerk Betty Jung, who coined "JAW's Prayer" (Grant Me Patience, Lord, But HURRY!) and kept my blood pressure down when I was in trial, and Frank Zolin, the fine executive officer of Superior Court, and a wonderful friend.

There are also those who shaped my life as a human being, guided me in growing up, whose touch still lingers at every crossroads of my life, telling me the direction to take. My great-grandmother Sarah, my grandmother Anna, my grandfather Samuel, and my uncle Paddy who was my hero when I was a child: you may be absent, but you are never gone.

Likewise, my thoughts are forever with "Dad Neb," Jimmy Nebenzahl, my father-in-law, who died in 1951, far too soon. You were a gem. My "Mom Nebenzahl" has been generous and supportive, and inspirational since I have known her. She calls me her "son-in-love" and I feel the same way about her. To all of the Nebenzahl clan, Harry, Bernie, Berty, Marilyn, and Nancy, brothers and sisters all, thanks.

What could possibly be adequate thanks to my mother and father or to my sister Irene? Just my deep gratitude forever. For my brother-in-law Russ, and my aunts Esther, Mary, and Rose, thanks also for caring. When I was bumping around the Pacific during the war, I wrote to Rose and asked her for an air mattress. She sent a telegram saying ". . . blondes are easier to find than air mattresses . . ." but find it she did, and I used it throughout the war except when I was in combat, and I have not forgotten.

The future for me is largely my children, as they have been so much of the past. Fred, David, and Sarah, thank you for being so large a part of my life, and thanks to my daughter-in-law, more like a daughter, Edna, and gratitude to my grandchildren, Gabriel and Ariel, for the continuity of life.

I am a judge. There are thousands of other judges in this country. Any one of them could have told stories like mine, or perhaps better. Each of them has his own view of what law is and what man is. These men and women toil constantly, often in very difficult conditions, to protect the core of our democracy, the law. I am always mindful of the honor of being in their ranks.

I was singled out from among them because I was asked to be on a wonderful TV show, the making of which is an unending pleasure. For that I thank particularly Ralph Edwards and Stu Billett, who gave me a chance to "do my thing."

There would have been no book without the encouragement of Michael Korda and Joni Evans, who had confidence that I could wield a typewriter as well as a gavel. Once begun, this book would have been difficult if not impossible without the brilliant insights of Ben Stein.

Frank Mankiewicz was the first to seriously suggest that I write a book. We have been friends for almost forty years and his belief in me has touched me for all that time.

I also thank Jeff Berg, the head of ICM, my fine agency, and Luis Sanjurjo, who worked as my agent, and who died tragically and untimely while this book was being written. Luis, you too are not forgotten.

At the most immediate level of support, thanks to Suzanne Ackerman, who works as a secretary and alter ego, for her loyalty and effectiveness.

Finally, above all, in love, family, friendship, devotion, intelligence, energy, everything important in every area of my life, love and thanks to my wife Mickey, the guiding star of my life. Thank you for helping me with every line of this book and every moment of my life, since we met long ago on a perfect day.

CONTENTS

A VIEW
FROM THE
BENCH

INTRODUCTION

Feeling Pain

*T*HE GLORY OF AMERICA is that we are a nation governed by laws and not by the whims and caprices of men and women. But the glory of American law is that it has room in it for the best qualities of men and women. In fact, our American way of justice cannot be separated from the qualities of empathy, intelligence, compassion, deliberation, and courage that men and women bring to it. The human qualities of judges, lawyers, plaintiffs, defendants, and witnesses, and men and women of the juries of America at their fullest are what make the justice system of this country able to respond to every detail and nuance, every grand stroke of human interaction that takes human beings into law courts.

Of course, all of the unfortunate characteristics of human nature—the greed, anger, jealousy, stupidity, small-mindedness, laziness, and just plain meanness of the human animal are also to be found in the law. After all, the life of the law is not logic, but experience, and experience of life at that.

In early 1973, a middle-aged woman whom I will call Carol Swanson (although she certainly lacked the grace of a swan) stepped out of her Dodge Dart in a parking lot in downtown Los Angeles, only a block or two from the famous City Hall building that used to be the backdrop to the titles in "Dragnet." Ms. Swanson had just arrived in town from Oakland and was in a hurry to check into her room in the motel. She slammed her car door, then walked quickly out of the parking lot toward the sidewalk. The weather was perfectly clear, as it almost always is in Los Angeles.

Unfortunately for Ms. Swanson, she made a mistake. Just as she reached the curb, she failed to notice a concrete parking barrier about eight inches off the ground. It had been put there to keep cars from rolling accidentally into Second Street. It was partially obscured—but only partially—by cars parked in front of it.

Ms. Swanson's toe caught the top of the barrier. Her forward momentum threw her forward. As she tried to regain her footing, her foot became twisted in the space between the barrier and the pavement. She fell to the sidewalk with a tragic thud. Her ankle was broken.

Paramedics came and took her to County–USC Medical Center. After she was diagnosed, set, and medicated for pain, her first call was to her lawyer.

She sued the owner and operator of the motel for negligently placing the barrier where an innocent woman might easily trip over it. Her claim, in other words, was that a careful woman or man would not see the barrier and would be likely to be tripped by it. The barrier was a sort of trap, so to speak, according to her.

Naturally, Ms. Swanson did not claim that the parking lot operator had set a trap like a guerrilla fighter filling a ditch with sharp sticks and then covering it up. Rather, Ms.

Swanson said that the parking lot operator had been negligent. The law will act against negligence at a certain level by awarding damages to whoever is harmed by that negligence. That was what Ms. Swanson wanted: not to put the motel operator in jail, but to be paid by him for her medical costs, and most importantly, she sought a much larger sum for her pain and suffering. Again, the law will often recompense a man or woman who has suffered through another's severe negligence by awarding not only money for the out-of-pocket costs of the injured person, but also an extra sum to make the plaintiff whole for her pain and suffering.

The owner of the motel had an entirely different view of the Swanson ankle, as you might expect. Judges rarely get to hear cases in which the plaintiff and the defendant agree, and trial judges never get to see cases where the plaintiff and the defendant agree on all the facts of an accident.

The defendant, whom I will call Cooper Motel, blamed most of the broken ankle on Ms. Swanson. Yes, said the defendant, perhaps we did have that parking lot barrier a trifle higher than it should have been. Yes, perhaps, just maybe it was a tiny bit obscured by the cars parked next to it. But any careful woman would have noticed it anyway, said Cooper. An ordinarily careful woman would not walk into a concrete barrier in broad daylight.

Therefore, Ms. Swanson was herself negligent in a way that the law calls "contributory negligence," said Cooper Motel. That is, she "contributed" to the general negligence of the situation that caused an accident, said the defendant. There is rarely an accident without either willfulness or negligence.

Under California law at the time, in a lawsuit such as Ms.

Swanson's, contributory negligence was a complete bar to winning the case. If a jury found that Ms. Swanson was contributorily negligent in the slightest degree, she simply lost. (The law has since been changed to a percentage formula of liability and damages known as "comparative negligence.")

Prior to trial, both sides were invited to see me in my chambers in the Superior Court and they told me their stories. Then an insurance adjuster representing the insurer of Cooper Motel came to see me with defense counsel. "Ms. Swanson has no case," he said, as insurance adjusters often say. "But just because we don't know what a jury will do, we'll give her five thousand to settle."

I had tried a great many personal injury cases. Frankly, Ms. Swanson's case was far from the strongest case I had ever seen. She did trip over a visible concrete barrier in broad daylight. The offer of five thousand dollars seemed like a very fair offer indeed.

I called in Ms. Swanson and her attorney. Interestingly, she was still limping painfully almost one year after the cast had been removed. "This is an excellent offer," I said. "I recommend that you save the taxpayers and yourself a great deal of trouble, avoid the risk of losing the case, and settle."

Ms. Swanson was aghast. She sat up straight in the chair in front of me and said, "Absolutely not. How can you even suggest such a thing?"

"I can suggest it because if the jury agrees with the defense about contributory negligence, you'll walk out of this courtroom without a penny," I said.

But Ms. Swanson leaped to her feet, forgetting her limp for a moment, and virtually shrieked at me. "How can you possibly presume to tell me to settle this case?'' she demanded. *''You can't feel my pain.''*

''Yes,'' I said to her after a few moments of thought, ''but I have had my own pain, and I know what pain feels like.''

In those few moments, my brain had taken me on a long, painful journey back almost thirty years and eight thousand miles across the Pacific to a time when pain was almost all I could feel.

Ms. Swanson's comment threw me back to Cebu City, Cebu, the Philippines, on April 10, 11, and 12, 1945. I was a lieutenant in the United States Army, serving in the 132nd Infantry of the Americal Division (the only division in the U.S. Army with a name instead of a number, named for America and New Caledonia, where it saw incredibly bitter fighting earlier in the war). My unit had landed on Cebu a few days before, taken the main city, Cebu, and was now advancing on the ring of hills that surrounded the town on three sides.

The Japanese were dug into those hills with great tenacity. They had built honeycombed tunnels and bunkers, reinforced with wood timbers and steel beams. They took twenty-millimeter automatic cannon from damaged Zeroes and adapted them to fire off tracks down onto the American forces. These cannon were loaded to fire phosphorous tracers which exploded into very hard, hot fragments on impact. Plus, the Japanese were themselves the most determined, battle-hardened foe imaginable.

I had already had an almost unbelievably lucky brush with a Japanese sniper only two days before. As I was crossing a rice paddy, I felt a slight thump in my knapsack and saw bullets kick up water all around me. Once I reached dry land, I saw that a Japanese Erisaka bullet had ripped into my poncho, through my knapsack, and been stopped only by a tin of tuna fish that my mother had sent to me and I hadn't gotten around to eating. (Thank you, Mom!)

On April 10, we were trying to clear the Japanese defenders out of a well-fortified hill called, blandly enough, Hill 26. Unfortunately, the action was anything but dull. My platoon medic was caught in devastating Japanese fire. He was hit in the chest and went down. Immediately, the Japanese fired incendiary tracers into the dry grass around him. The grass went up in flames. The helpless corporal was about to be enveloped in fire.

I crawled out, joined by a rifleman, wondering what on earth I was doing there, and we dragged the man back to safety, under constant sniper and machine-gun fire. But meanwhile, our unit was pinned down and isolated.

Just as I had been taught to do, I started digging a trench with my bayonet and my shovel. Suddenly, the Japanese opened up again with their damned twenty-millimeter tracers all around me.

I felt an excruciating pain in my foot, in my legs, and in my spine. It was an entirely new order of pain from anything I had ever known about until that day. I had been hit by phosphorus and shrapnel. Almost immediately afterward, the Japanese attacked with one of their justly feared banzai attacks.

For an entire night, Company I was surrounded by attacking Japanese. Our men fought back even harder, and through the whole night I could hear the screams of men on both sides who had been shot. The company medic gave me four shots of morphine, but still the pain in my spine and foot and the terror of the battle kept me awake.

When we had finally repelled the attack, Filipino stretcher-bearers came to carry the wounded, including yours truly, back to a field hospital in Cebu City. As luck would have it, just as the Filipinos reached the main path, the Japanese again opened up on us with those twenty-millimeter guns and machine guns. The stretcher-bearers simply dropped us on the path and ran for cover. For most of the morning, we lay exposed to Japanese fire, barely able to crawl.

When the shooting finally let up, after what seemed like an eternity of machine-gun fire, torrential rain, and death, the stretcher-bearers came back and finally got us to the Cebu field hospital. I was operated on for my back and foot and eventually carried into a recovery tent. As I drifted in and out of consciousness, I recall hearing grown men sobbing. Then I heard a nurse tell me, through tears, that Franklin Roosevelt was dead.

Men who had seen the most bloody combat in the Pacific wept like small children. It was as if our own hurt had suddenly been put on the back burner while we felt that pain of the whole nation and the whole world about FDR. Of all of the agony of those horrible three days, the bottom-falling-out news of FDR was the most lingering of all.

When Ms. Swanson told me I could not possibly feel her pain, all of that came back to me like an unwelcome thunderclap.

Now, I bring all of this up not to boast about my war wounds. Many, many men and women were far braver than I was. Many of them never came back at all or came back horribly, grotesquely wounded.

The point of the story is not about spinal injuries or about twenty-millimeter tracer fire or about brave men dying on

Hill 26. On that night when I felt so much of my own pain, and then the pain of my men dying and getting maimed around me, and then the pain of FDR's death, I realized that a great deal of life is exactly and precisely about being able to feel pain, my own and other people's.

Humanity starts, I sometimes think, when one human being can empathize with another's pain. That empathy, carried into action, can only mean that humans take steps to lessen other people's pain, and that is what civilization and mercy and humanity are all about. And, to get back to Ms. Swanson, that is a large part of what being a judge is all about.

The ability of a judge to put himself into the shoes of the men and women who appear before him is the heart of being a decent judge. And while I cannot lay claim to being the best judge in history, I can and do claim to have been a decent judge, and to have felt other people's pain.

Again, the ability to sympathize and empathize with others' suffering is important in any field. It is key to being a human being with any claim to humanity.

But for a judge, the quality of sensing others' pain is crucial. Men and women do not come to court unless they have felt some kind of loss, be it physical or emotional or financial. Plaintiffs and defendants are usually hurting from that loss. If a judge cannot understand litigants who are feeling pain, he will never be able to comprehend the essence of a case or what is fair or unfair in the context of the people involved. The law on the books is about resolving pain and conflict in the abstract. Judges make it happen in the flesh. If they cannot feel for the people in front of them, they should be in another job.

This book then is about what it has been like for me to have been a judge for twenty years on the bench of the Municipal and Superior courts, Los Angeles, California, from 1959 to 1979 and to have tried to put myself into the loss and anger and dismay of the people who appeared before me, and then to have given them that precious gift—simple justice.

But these are not stories of pain for the most part. It is a happy, wonderful fact of life in this country that we can and do dispense justice to people who feel wronged. It is an occasion for pride and satisfaction that we have a system for offering justice that takes into account the feelings of the ordinary citizen in his car or her beauty shop or in a school or in an office or in a bedroom or in a prison. Everyone who lives in this country should feel proud that our system strives to give consideration not just to the autocratic feelings of a judge, but to the complaints and fears of a bookkeeper or a retiree or a nurse or a mill hand or a farmer.

Naturally, a judge should not decide a case on the basis of empathy, sympathy or passion. He must weigh the evidence, compare it with the requirements of the law, and then dispense justice without regard to his personal prejudices. But to understand the case, he must be able to understand the people in the case.

The fact of human conflict is an inevitable fact of human nature. The facts of accidents and crimes are basic facts of human interaction—although even made worse by circumstances beyond individuals' control. But the fact that Joe Wapner, and thousands of other judges, offer justice with reference to needs of the ordinary American without regard to wealth or skin color or political affiliation for the most part is a great accomplishment of this country and this people. With rare exceptions judges in America feel for the people who come before them. Those people are not just pawns to be moved about for the convenience of some political party or one's boss or supposedly perfect cause. This, too, is a great fact of the American justice system, and something for us all to rejoice about.

When Americans leave a courtroom feeling that their cries have been heard, we should all share pride in the fact that our legal system works as well as it does.

This is what these stories are about: the law, the men and women who come before the law, how justice gets meted out in funny and sad ways, how the system sometimes fails, and why, but most of all, how one judge—no better than many other judges—tried to put empathy and his basic feelings for people into meting out simple justice. These are not stories of complex legal maneuverings or deep legal theories. They are stories of ordinary people, an ordinary judge, and a feeling between them that led—I hope—to something far more than ordinary in this world—justice. I am not claiming that the judicial system is perfect, by any means. There are large problems of delays, cumbersome procedures, the rare but troublesome lack of ethics in the bar, and all of the human mistakes made in a system created by humans and run by humans just like everybody else.

By the way, Ms. Swanson did indeed turn down the settlement I suggested. The case went to trial before a jury. After hearing all of the evidence, the jury retired to reach a verdict. After only a few hours, the jury returned with a statement that Ms. Swanson was indeed not entitled to recover any damages. Her own negligence in failing to see a concrete barrier in broad daylight was a complete bar to recovery, said the jurors.

Ms. Swanson, sitting at the plaintiff's table, went pale. "Does this mean I don't get any money?" she asked.

"It means exactly that," I answered.

"Then I'll take the five thousand you offered a few days ago," she said in a rush.

"I'm sorry," I said. "You already turned that down. It's not available after you've lost the case."

Ms. Swanson was stunned. She walked away empty-handed. In a way, I felt sorry for her, but in a way, she had brought it on herself. She rolled the dice. She could possibly have won. But she lost. My greatest regret about Ms. Swanson is that she did not realize that I could feel her pain.

CHAPTER ONE

The House
of Justice

*F*or almost forty years, a man and woman of modest circumstances lived in a neat, well-kept bungalow south of Wilshire Boulevard in Los Angeles, not far from the once-modern office buildings of the "Miracle Mile." The husband was a school custodian for the Los Angeles public school system. The wife kept house and raised children, let's say. To save hurt feelings, I will call them Mr. and Mrs. Scott.

Sometime in 1975, Mr. Scott, by then retired, died suddenly. Mrs. Scott was left with the proceeds of a tiny insurance policy and her house, which was fully paid for. She had never had to keep track of bills and paperwork, and she knew no accountants. She probably could not have afforded one anyway.

Not more than a few months after Mr. Scott died, the city of Los Angeles began to repair and repave Wilshire Boulevard to make it into a larger, more commercially viable street. Under a law passed by the Los Angeles City Council in 1911, when street improvements are made, all of the property owners in the neighborhood are responsible for paying an assessment to cover costs.

Accordingly, a letter from the city went out to Mr. and Mrs. Scott. The letter was in almost incomprehensible legalese. It talked about "resolutions" and "bond assessments" and payments on "debentures." Frankly, when I eventually saw it, I could barely follow it myself. Mrs. Scott had a difficult enough time with the bills from credit cards and department stores. She apparently assumed that the complex bill was a form letter without any meaning in her life and ignored it.

About one year later, another letter went out from the city to Mrs. Scott. This time, the letter was filled with talk about "bondholders," "delinquency notices," and "interest recapture." A copy of the letter, typed neatly enough for the city bureaucracy, was sent to the last school that the already deceased Mr. Scott had worked at, where it was promptly thrown away.

Mrs. Scott did nothing in response to either letter.

About six months after that, a notice came to Mrs. Scott informing her (without ever mentioning her street address) that unless there was a payment of a coupon to bondholder serial number blankety-blank a city agency would mandate the sale of certain parcels, including about twenty lots and parcel numbers.

Almost simultaneously with the receipt of that last dense ball of bureaucratese, Mrs. Scott became ill herself and went into the hospital for about eight weeks with a severe pneumonia. While she was in the hospital, another letter came, announcing a sale for delinquency of bond payments of certain parcel numbers. For a perfect touch, a copy of that letter was also sent to the last school where Mr. Scott had worked.

When Mrs. Scott came home from the hospital, she

recuperated for a few weeks. Then one day a carefully groomed businessman appeared at her front door. The man, whom I will call Mr. Osborne, handed Mrs. Scott a notice to quit. "Your property was sold to me for the back street-repairs assessment plus interest," he said. "I'm planning to renovate this house and then sell it. I'm afraid you'll have to move out."

Mrs. Scott, as you might imagine, was amazed. She dragged herself to City Hall, where she learned more amazing facts. First, all of those notices about bondholders were really the equivalent of notices of a tax. Second, those notices about unpaid bondholders and missed coupons were about back taxes due.

Third, as an unsmiling clerk later testified in my court, those parcel numbers included her house. Fourth, strictly in conformity with the 1911 law on street-repair assessments, her home had been sold for the amount of her street-repair assessments, which was about eleven hundred dollars. (Her house was worth about fifty thousand dollars on the open market.) Mr. Osborne was a property developer specializing in buying distressed properties at bargain prices. He had done everything according to Hoyle, and by every precedent of law as it is written down in law books, the house was now his. He could do with it as he chose.

Mrs. Scott was not about to leave the house she had lived in for forty years, where she had spent the whole of her marriage. She found a lawyer who would represent her for almost zero—which was what she could afford. She refused to leave her house, and her lawyer filed papers challenging Mr. Osborne's claim to title of her house.

The case came before me as the driest, most clear-cut legal matter of the month: a property owner had not paid the equivalent of taxes. Another citizen had strictly followed the law. He had paid the money she owed the city. By every statute I could find, the house was his. He could order her to leave it so he could have it renovated, and he could—so the 1911 law specified—have marshals of the court evict her and her belongings. This was cut and dried.

However, I did not quite see it that way. What I saw was not a "property owner," or a "tax delinquent." Mrs. Scott was a woman who had done her best to be a responsible member of society. She had never had a brush with the law. She had raised two children, both of whom were fully productive adults with children of their own. She had never been prepared, by her husband or anyone else, to cope with the incredibly bizarre, complex verbiage of the city of Los Angeles about bonds and coupons. She was no longer young. She was not in good health. The only thing that rooted her to society and made her feel as if she belonged was her house. The woman I saw before me was innocent and deserving of the law's protection.

Nevertheless. Mr. Osborne stood in front of me in his well-pressed gray suit, with his lawyer, also in a well-pressed gray suit, and made his points. He had complied with the law. What did the law mean if not that following the rules was what counted? If a property owner could not feel secure after he had paid his money to the city and gotten a deed from the city, what did property rights mean? How could any property owner or self-respecting businessman ever feel secure in dealing with city laws again if Mr. Osborne did not get to have clear title to that house?

For me, to be honest, the decision was not difficult. As I watched and listened, I started to get so angry that my longtime clerk, Betty Jung, handed me a quick sketch of a thermometer reaching the boiling point on which she had written, "Cool down."

"Mr. Osborne," I said, "the law is not intended to be used to throw an innocent woman out of her home. You have not done anything wrong, and basically there are two innocent people here. But one of them has a profit at stake. Another one has her home at stake. I will not under any circumstances order that woman evicted from her home. She must pay the street assessment, and you will get repaid what you paid, plus interest. But I order title to be vested in Mrs. Scott."

As you might imagine, Mr. Osborne became agitated indeed. "What you are doing is not the law," his lawyer said condescendingly.

"The law is not that a woman gets thrown out of her house because she could not follow bureaucratic double-talk and some notices got mailed to the wrong address," I said. "If you want, go ahead and appeal. Maybe some other court will overrule me and throw this woman out of her home. To this judge, the law doesn't mean that. Not in my court."

I did not blame Mr. Osborne or find him an unusual specimen of humanity. The sad fact is that a great many human beings are content to make a profit out of kicking an innocent man or woman out of a home. That was how he made his living. But I was not about to lend the moral decisiveness of the law to his values.

Legalisms about bondholders and procedure for notice are important parts of the nation's jurisprudence. But safeguarding the only home of deserving people is the very essence of justice.

Mr. Osborne took me at my word. He did indeed appeal.

Twice. Once the case got bounced back to me for a brief hearing about whether the notice provisions were valid. That is, I was asked to find out whether Mrs. Scott had her property taken away from her without due process of law, which is strictly forbidden by the Constitution.

As you might expect, I found that mailing a jumble of confusing notices did not amount to any meaningful warning to Mrs. Scott that her home was about to be sold out from under her.

The Appeals Court backed me up. Twice. They found that the 1911 law was constitutionally void because it did not provide for enough safeguards before people's homes were taken away from them. Since the case of Mrs. Scott, the law requires that property owners be told in plain English, with clear evidence that they understand what is going on, when a delinquent assessment against their homes is ordered. In Los Angeles, at least, there should never be any more cases like that of Mrs. Scott and Mr. Osborne.

This case never made the national press. It was just a local case about putting human compassion and just plain common sense into a law that was heartless. In Mrs. Scott's safe, quiet return to her home was a large win for what I see as the best of justice.

CHAPTER TWO

Seeing Things

*B*efore Governor Edmund G. "Pat" Brown appointed me to the Superior Court, I was for two years a judge of the Municipal Court of Los Angeles. In that court, I tried the cases of daily life: traffic tickets, small claims, errant dogs and their owners.

On my very first day in that court, working at Eighth and Wall streets in downtown Los Angeles, I had a case that gave me a chance to put myself into the law. A man in late middle age, whom I will call Mr. Tobin, appeared before me in a brightly checked sport jacket and the loudest electric blue trousers I have ever seen before or since. He looked like a circus barker.

But when his case was called, Mr. Tobin turned out to be a pleasant, mild-mannered, polite man. The charge against him was that he had driven his car sixty-five miles per hour in a thirty-five-mile zone on Olympic Boulevard. A policeman said he had followed Mr. Tobin's 1949 Cadillac and clocked it at sixty. That, as far as the policeman was concerned, should have ended the case. Mr. Tobin politely but firmly disagreed.

"Your Honor," Mr. Tobin said, "my car is broken. It's

been broken for three years. It won't even go over thirty-five. I can't take it on the freeway, couldn't get it to go over thirty-five if my life depended on it.''

The policeman laughed out loud. When I asked him about the car, he said that whatever Mr. Tobin might have claimed, he had clocked the car at sixty. "Anyway," he said, "I have yet to see the Cadillac that won't go over thirty-five.''

"All right," I said to Mr. Tobin. "If you'll wait until I finish with my other cases, I'll ride in your car myself. If it won't go over thirty-five, you win.''

Mr. Tobin patiently waited most of the day for me to get through my calendar. Then, just before the evening rush hour, I ducked out with my bailiff, Dick Mansfield (this was before the days of Rusty Burrell, but Dick was also a fine bailiff). The bailiff sat in the driver's seat. Mr. Tobin sat in the passenger's seat. I sat in the backseat, and away we went, also on Olympic Boulevard.

No matter how far the bailiff pressed down on the accelerator, no matter how long a start we had, that car would not go over thirty-five. It had a broken early automatic transmission, and it would simply not allow the engine to engage the wheels fully.

I took Mr. Tobin back to court, banged my gavel very lightly, and said, "Not guilty.''

Mr. Tobin and his car taught me an invaluable lesson: Put your own eyes and ears and good sense into the case before you. Don't trust others when your own common sense is telling you that something is wrong. Look for the truth of a case with your own eyes. The law is not supposed to be run like a machine, with inanimate facts being put in one end and an inanimate verdict coming out the other end. The law has a person there to enforce it and render judgments. Let that *person* have something to say.

About six months later, when I was nearing the end of my tenure in Traffic Court, I had a similar experience. A man appeared before me, charged with running a stop sign in Hancock Park. Hancock Park is one of the oldest, most elegant neighborhoods in Los Angeles. It has magnificent tree-lined blocks with enormous Spanish and Tudor and Colonial houses behind the sloping lawns. Mr. Robins, as I will call him, was charged with running a stop sign on the exact block where Mrs. Buffy Chandler, who owns a large part of the *Los Angeles Times,* has her mansion.

The policeman testified about seeing the "crime" and then left the stand. "The fact is," said Mr. Robins, a man who looked like the high-school gym teacher he was, with a ruddy face and deliberate, stolid movements, "that there simply is no stop sign on that corner. I have been going by that corner for five years, and there never has been a stop sign."

Even to me, who tries to look at every case from every angle, that seemed farfetched.

"I'll tell you what," said Mr. Robins. "I'll write out a check right now for fifty dollars to any charity you mention if you'll just go look at that corner. If there's a stop sign, I'll pay the fine and you give the check to your favorite charity. If there's no stop sign, you give the check to your charity anyway."

Mr. Robins did not appear to be a wealthy man. For him to offer fifty dollars—in a day when a dollar was the equivalent of five dollars today—that I'm sure meant a great deal to him and it certainly impressed me.

I told Mr. Robins I would send out my trusty bailiff

immediately after the docket was done. The policeman glow-ered at me, but I overlooked it. A judge should not be swayed by dirty looks from either policemen or accused felons.

No sooner had I made that arrangement with Mr. Robins than another defendant in a stop-sign case made the exact same request. He also insisted that there was no stop sign, this time at an intersection in the Hollywood Hills. One thing judges strive to do is enforce the law equally to defendants in similar situations. I therefore made the same agreement with the second defendant as well. Both men duly made out their checks to City of Hope, a research hospital in Southern California. Then they waited for the bailiff to make his report.

Sure enough, there was no stop sign at either corner. Both defendants left with honor satisfied and with the pride of knowing they had contributed to a good cause. As for the policemen, I hope they learned something about not con-fusing their authority to enforce the law with the right to enforce their own mistakes as if they were the law.

About three years later, when I was on the Superior Court, I had a case which was far more serious than those traffic cases, but required the same placement of the human mind and human sense into a situation where dry recitations would have mocked the Constitution.

A husband and wife whom I will call Mr. and Mrs. Ray were known to the police in the Rampart Division to be serious heroin users. The couple had served time in a state penitentiary, and also in County Jail, for possession of heroin. Now they were out, and a detective on the narcotics squad of the Los Angeles Police Department had been following them.

One day in 1963, the policeman followed them to a ramshackle, pitifully dilapidated motel–apartment house on the corner of Twelfth and Hill, in a sad neighborhood just south of downtown Los Angeles. As he later testified, the policeman waited for a few minutes outside the apartment. Then, as he claimed, he looked through the keyhole of the apartment door without being noticed by Mr. and Mrs. Ray.

He saw, as he testified in my court later in 1963, that Mr. and Mrs. Ray took heroin out of a glassine envelope, heated it with a candle, put it into a syringe, and then took turns injecting each other with it.

"When I saw that," said the detective, "I broke down the door, went inside, and arrested the two of them."

The defendants' lawyer, Sam Bubrick, a very capable criminal defense lawyer, came before me. "I won't deny that my clients use heroin," he said. "I won't deny that they were under the influence of heroin when they were arrested. What I do say is that they were arrested as a result of an illegal search and seizure. That policeman could not possibly have seen anything more than the floor through the keyhole. He just broke down the door on a guess. He had no reasonable basis for believing that he would find anything, and no probable cause for his search and seizure."

The attorney was so sure that the search had been unlawful that he waived trial by jury. He would not rely on theatrics or a confused juror. He wanted me to go myself to the apartment and look through the keyhole. "If you can see anything, if you can see what two people were doing on the couch, my clients will plead guilty," he said.

Now it is crucial to understand something: Generally speaking, I have the highest regard for policemen, and especially for the LAPD. They risk their lives to protect civilians every hour of every day. They get paid poorly. They do not acquire the glittering Porsches and houses in Beverly Hills that people who perform far less worthwhile services acquire without ever risking anything more than indigestion. But policemen are human beings, just like defendants or like judges. They make mistakes, too. They have every human motivation that anyone else has, including the wish to take shortcuts, especially when they are dealing with known drug users. I have great respect for the police, but they are not perfect.

Also, as a judge, and as an American, I have a virtual obsession with law and order. This country is great in large measure because it follows law instead of following the vagaries of human nature, and because it provides an orderly arena for men and women to work, play, take care of their families and themselves, and make progress.

But for me, as for anyone who knows the history of this country, "law and order" begins with everyone following the Constitution—and I mean *everyone*, from policemen to presidents.

Under the Constitution, the citizens of America are guaranteed certain vital rights as free people. The Fourth Amendment to the Constitution provides for one of the most basic rights:

> The right of the people to be secure in their persons, houses, papers, and effects, against unreasonable searches and seizures, shall not be violated, and no warrants shall issue, but upon probable cause, supported by oath or affirmation, and particularly describing the place to be searched, and the persons or things to be seized.

These are not empty words. They tell Americans that no one, not police or FBI or anyone, can lawfully disturb their peace and security except when there is *probable cause* to believe that a crime has been committed or is about to be committed or in clear pursuit of solving a crime. Without the Fourth Amendment, we would all know much less peace of mind.

As I saw it, the Fourth Amendment applies just as fully to Mr. and Mrs. Ray in their miserable apartment in downtown Los Angeles as it does to a millionaire living in a palace in Bel Air. If it did not, we would no longer be a nation of laws.

I thought about all of this, and I agreed to the lawyer's suggestion. The defendants, their attorney, the prosecutor, the witness, the bailiff, the clerk, the court reporter, and I all went to the apartment on Twelfth and Hill. The policeman placed the defendants inside the apartment in the positions where he said they were. Then we all took turns crouching on the dusty hallway floor and looking through the keyhole.

When it was my turn, there was absolutely no doubt about it. All I could see was a few feet of the floor in front of the keyhole. That was all anyone could see.

"Wait," the police detective said. "I made a mistake. They were at the table, not the couch."

"All right," I said. "Let's move them to the table where you now say they were."

The defendants moved to the table, and again, we all went in the hallway and peeked through the keyhole. We still could not see any human beings or any table. All we could see was the floor.

Our cavalcade went back to Department 117, where I was

then holding my court. The defense lawyer made a motion to dismiss the case because the evidence used by the prosecution had been seized pursuant to an illegal search and seizure

ı granted the motion.

Again, I certainly did not endorse Mr. and Mrs. Ray's way of life and death. Illegal drugs are a curse in this country, ripping us apart and killing the spirit of many people of all ages.

But I was not going to let drugs claim as a victim the Constitution of the United States. That would not be law. It would be vigilantism and lawlessness.

From Mr. Tobin's Cadillac that would not go over thirty-five, I had learned the lesson of interjecting my own eyes and ears into a case. In Mr. Tobin's day in court, it saved him from a speeding fine. For Mr. and Mrs. Ray, that same habit gave them—and the rest of us—the protection of the Constitution.

CHAPTER THREE

The Heart of the City

*J*ohnny Archer was by no means a lucky young man when he came before me in 1965. He had been born in a sharecropper's cabin outside Ozark, Alabama. He dropped out of high school at the age of fifteen to work at a feed lot in Ozark, Alabama. Then he had a really bad stroke of luck. When he was eighteen, someone told him he was handsome. The same informant told Archer that he was handsome enough to be a movie star, and that he should take himself to Hollywood, where he would undoubtedly get to be a movie star his very own self.

Sadly for him, Archer took the kind words seriously. He thought about them until he was twenty. Then he cashed his weekly paycheck and bought a Greyhound ticket to Los Angeles.

Naturally, when he made the rounds of the studios, he got absolutely nowhere. He could hardly believe that no one at all wanted him to be a movie star, not even a small movie star. Not only that, but there were no big movie starlets waiting to fall in love with him either. He was barely able to get a job as a dishwasher and a room at a flophouse on Ivar Street off Hollywood Boulevard.

He was so distressed that he could only stay in his job for a week. Then he moved out of the flophouse and decided that he had better go back down South. He stood on the shoulder of the Hollywood Freeway access ramp for an hour and no one gave him a ride. He was tired and depressed. Finally, a man came by in a new Volkswagen Rabbit and smilingly asked Archer where he was planning to go.

"I want to go down South," he said.

"Perfect," the driver said.

In fact, the driver was not heading "down South" as Archer understood it, which would have meant Alabama. Rather, he was heading "down South" to Mexico, and for a good reason. He had just stolen the Volkswagen Rabbit and wanted to take it to Tijuana to sell it for spare parts.

A California highway patrolman flagged down the Rabbit for speeding just before the Harbor Freeway exit. Of course, the driver soon found himself under arrest for car theft and for using a car without the owner's permission.

Johnny Archer, who did not give a particularly convincing explanation of his presence in the stolen car since he was asleep when the car was pulled over, was booked for car theft and unauthorized use as well.

When Johnny Archer came before me in Superior Court, his luck started to change. Most important for him, he got a young lawyer named Armand Arabian as his defense counsel. Armand Arabian, then trying his first case before me, is now a justice of the California Court of Appeals.

The case was tried in the old Brunswig Drug Company building, which was a dark and miserable place even on a sunny day. On the day of Johnny Archer's trial, one of Los Angeles' rare downpours was whipping all around the building, giving it a Gothic, frightening look.

Still, it was the perfect setting for Arabian's speech to the jury. He told them forcefully that Archer was not in any way criminally involved with the theft of the car. "Not only that," he said, "but this young man, whom you see before you, has to his name only the pair of jeans he is wearing, his torn white shirt, one pair of shoes, and one pair of socks. His only crime is poverty and ignorance."

The speech worked wonders. Not only was Archer acquitted, but the jury, while deliberating, took up a collection for him. They called the Greyhound terminal to find out how much a bus ticket back to Ozark, Alabama, would be, and then collected it among themselves to give to Johnny Archer, to get him back to a place where he could cope more easily with real life.

When I saw and heard what the jurors had done, a feeling I had about Archer jelled inside me as well. "What size are you?" I asked him as he stood before the bench.

"Around a forty," he said.

"All right," I said. "The jury has found you not guilty. I have no further legal jurisdiction over you. This is a Friday. But I order you to stay in jail until Monday, and then I'll see about sending you back home with your head held high."

I went home, confident, or at least hoping, that Archer would not get into any further trouble over the weekend. I found a suit that was still serviceable, a shirt, socks, and a tie. I could not give him my shoes, because I wear special orthopedic shoes because of the twenty-millimeter tracer fragments still in my foot.

But on Monday, I called Archer before me and gave him my former clothes, the jury's bus ticket, and my contribution of money for shoes. "As soon as you get your shoes,"

I said, "I suggest you head back home. I'm sure your friends miss you."

Johnny Archer went back home, and I hope he ignores the next man who tells him he's handsome enough to be a movie star.

As for Armand Arabian, to this day he tells our mutual friends that on his first case before Joe Wapner, he not only got his client off, but he got the shirt off the judge's back.

CHAPTER FOUR

What Neighborhood Means

I was not always a judge. When I was a child, I lived in a middle-class neighborhood not far from downtown. On North Kenmore Avenue. If you visit that area today, you will see the campus of Los Angeles City College, one of the largest community colleges in America. But when I lived there, in the 1920s and early 1930s, it was simply a quiet neighborhood.

Our family knew every other family within half a mile, and maybe more. The children all played and went to school with one another. The adults and parents all discussed the news of the day together. If anyone needed a cup of milk, or a sympathetic ear, there were neighbors to provide. If tough kids from out of the neighborhood came by to make trouble, the kids from our block would all rally around, even though the conflict was mostly confined to name-calling. (Gang violence as practiced today in Los Angeles was unknown.)

When my wife and I had our children, we lived in a neighborhood some distance from Kenmore Avenue, on Waterford Street, not far from the San Diego Freeway. There, too, we knew all of our neighbors. We would get together on Saturday for softball games in the summer or for football (touch, of course) in the fall. None of us was very good at either game, but we played together and we all had fun. If a boy or girl needed a ride to school and his parents were occupied, there was always someone there to lend a car and a friendly hand.

I am not Pollyanna, and I do not pretend that there were no quarrels in the neighborhood. Where human beings are close to one another, there will always be at least some acrimony.

But overall, both on Kenmore Avenue and on Waterford Street, neighbors realized that the value of neighborliness was worth attention, care, and a goodly measure of time. It was simply taken for granted that neighbors would give of their days and weeks and months to keep their neighborhoods as a force for better lives. It worked wonderfully, too. I was able to grow up with a feeling that I was in a sort of family as soon as I entered the neighborhood, and not just as I entered our home. Our sons and daughter were able to feel that they were always among friends anywhere near our house.

This gave a feeling of security which is necessary to make human beings into whole people with the inner strength to raise families and carry on with the business of love and life.

Somewhere, sometime, that all came grinding to a halt, at least in large parts of Los Angeles. From what I have been able to see, it has also come to a halt in large parts of America. About twenty years ago, maybe a little more or a little less, Americans came to the conclusion that they were too busy to spend any time with their neighbors. John and Jane Doe decided that it was more valuable to spend time working to save up for a sports car or working out at the health club or maybe just watching the world go by than to keep their neighborhoods going as viable places.

Maybe it had to do with the great inflations of the 1970s, when people were worried about money and decided to spend all of their time looking for more money. At least I have heard that suggestion. But then again, when I was a young man during the Great Depression, times were incomparably harder than they were in the 1970s, and yet neighbors clung together incredibly well. If anything, they grew stronger. Maybe it has to do with the amazing mobility of Americans. I have read that the average American family moves every three years. Perhaps that movement, supposedly for better jobs and better standards of living, has simply made the concept of neighborhoods a geographic and not an emotional one.

Maybe there are just so many more Americans than there were, with so many more cars and so many more airline tickets and so much to do, that personal contacts have simply become impossible to maintain in a geographically bound area such as a neighborhood.

For whatever reasons, neighborhoods, and the connections between people of trust and helpfulness that were once a staple of daily life in America, are far too often just a fantasy used by advertisers.

Make no mistake about it: This is a severe loss for America. When the glue of trust and appreciation in neighborhoods wears away, the same ties start to disappear in the larger society, and we are no longer the country we should be. We are not yet at that point, but the signs and portents are clear.

———

One of the most impressive neighborhoods of postwar Los Angeles was Baldwin Hills. It was set on a hill south of downtown and east of Beverly Hills. At night, it had sweeping views of the lights of downtown, and in some directions, one could see all the way to Catalina Island over the Pacific.

The neighborhood had a famous shopping center, Baldwin Hills Plaza, where families bought their clothes and food and candy. All of the neighbors had gotten together to write rules and procedures to protect the scenic beauty of the neighborhood, and there was a neighborhood association to make certain that the aesthetic beauty of the place was protected. Houses were required to be only a certain height so as not to block their neighbors' view, and maintenance of homes was strictly enforced, although the neighborly spirit of the place made legal enforcement unnecessary.

Then, in the early and mid-seventies, the neighborhood began to change drastically. Families moved in for the views but refused to observe the covenants about protecting the beauty of Baldwin Hills. Abandoned cars were left on the streets. Homeowners built second and third stories which ruined their neighbors' views. The neighborhood became polarized between the old and new residents of Baldwin Hills. Naturally, the older residents wanted to protect the neighborhood they had nurtured. The newer residents only wanted to "do their thing" without interference. If "doing their thing" meant changing the neighborhood for the worse—well, that was somebody else's problem. They saw their interests as confined to their own households. They were not willing to commit to some self-restraint for the betterment of their neighborhood.

The Baldwin Hills Community Preservation Committee

was formed by the more traditional neighbors to protect their area. This group noted that the covenants that supposedly bound all the neighbors allowed the imposition of a very small assessment—twenty-five cents per front foot—to collect money to beautify the community.

When the BHCPC mailed out the assessments, the newer neighbors often refused to pay. They formed a group of their own, and said that the covenants (or CC & Rs,* as they are often called) were illegal.

The BHCPC went to Superior Court and asked for a "declaratory judgment" on the CC & Rs. Under a declaratory judgment, a court is asked to decide whether a certain act or law is legal before an actual conflict is brought under law. In effect, a litigant is asking a court to "declare" whether a law is binding or what the legal status of a conflict is.

The case came before me. The first witness out of a list of dozens of witnesses appeared on the stand. He started to tell in great detail about the unsightly wrecks on the streets and how each jot and tittle of the CC & Rs applied to every possible aspect of life in Baldwin Hills.

I was appalled. Even though Betty Jung was doing her best to restrain me, and even though I had her special prayer for me to set up on the bench before me ("JAW's Prayer," it read. "Grant me patience, Lord, but HURRY!"), I could hardly control my anger.

"Do you people think I'm going to sit here for a week and listen to this nonsense? You people are neighbors. You bought your houses knowing very well that there were CC & Rs. You approved them. If you're neighbors, you can work this out." I directed the lawyers and the leaders of the

---

* CC & Rs are Codes, Covenants and Restrictions.

two factions to go into my conference room and not come out without a settlement.

"I live in a neighborhood," I added. "We have a homeowners' association. If we can work things out, you can work them out as well. *That's what being neighbors means.*"

The neighbors sheepishly went into the conference room and, when the doors closed, went after each other like demons. But after a few days of argument, and after many conferences with me, a rough compromise was reached. There were a few cosmetic plums for the dissidents, but basically the CC & Rs were enforced. The problem was that the neighbors who were in the conference room were afraid that they would not be able to sell the arrangement to the rank and file within the neighborhood.

"Your Honor," said one of the dissident leaders, "we can only make this fly if you will come to our neighborhood and explain it yourself."

"If that's what it takes to put your neighborhood back together," I said, "you've got yourself a judge."

Two weeks later, there was a cocktail party in a lovely Baldwin Hills home where the leaders of both factions gathered. Then there was a meeting of four hundred people from the neighborhood in a school auditorium. I made a presentation about the settlement and then answered questions for most of the night. Finally, almost everyone was satisfied. The agreement was put to a vote and passed resoundingly.

I wish I could say that the neighborhood was then returned to its former peace and loveliness. Unfortunately, there was still sporadic sniping against the settlement, sometimes led by a fellow judge who lived in the neighborhood. For several years longer, the neighborhood was attractive, and it still is one of the more appealing parts of residential Los Angeles. But the neighborly spirit was largely gone. This is exactly the point of the story.

An atmosphere of trust and self-restraint among neighbors is not a legally recognizable remedy. I could as a judge order injunctions or damages or specific performance in rare cases. ("Specific performance" is when a judge orders a litigant to do a particular act, usually such as signing a deed, or something related to real estate.) But no judge can order neighbors to have the same neighborly feelings that—I think—neighbors would have had in 1933 or even in 1963. Something valuable has been lost in our streets and blocks. I am not certain how we get it back, but I know that a judge cannot order it. Human feelings cannot be changed in a court of law. The effects of massive social dislocations cannot be remedied by a writ of Superior Court.

CHAPTER FIVE

Taking Chances

*E*ven in the day of collapsing neighborhoods and di-minished feelings of trust among Americans, there can still be oases of good feeling. The human spirit can still be nurtured by another human being reaching out to help, even when one of those human beings wears prison clothes and one wears black robes.

In 1963, Governor Pat Brown had a novel idea. He wanted Superior Court judges to visit California's prisons. The thought—and it was a good one—was that we should have an idea of what we were about when we sent men and women to prison, what their living conditions would be, and how their lives would be affected.

I took to the plan immediately. Any time that I can gain experience of real life to help me work with the abstract body of law, I jump at it. In early 1963, my wife, my children, and I took a driving vacation to see the major prisons of California. Our first stop was Atascadero State Prison, near San Luis Obispo. Atascadero is not simply a prison. It is a facility for the criminally insane. At Atascadero, the population includes a large number of child molesters, rapists, killers, drug addicts, and other men whose primary motivations for crime are not circumstance or hardship, but the working out of a mental illness.

These are, by and large, frightening people.

As the warden of Atascadero showed me around, I watched various prison activities—volleyball, reading, Ping-Pong, weight lifting, and forms of group psychological therapy. One of the most innovative groups centered around a group of inmates who are given certain rights of self-government within Atascadero, involving small details of prison rules and regulations. This was called ESP (not extra sensory perception but emotional security program).

On the day I was visiting Atascadero, the inmate running the ESP program was a man whom I will call James Vasquez. He was of medium height, with a sturdy profile. He carried himself like a six-footer despite his average height. He handled the meeting authoritatively but with diplomacy and tact. Clearly, this man was an executive, albeit an executive at a prison. I had been to many meetings of lawyers which were not handled as effectively as Vasquez handled his meeting.

When I returned to my court, I had the file on Mr. Vasquez pulled. To my surprise and dismay, I found that he had been sentenced to Atascadero by none other than Wapner, J.! When I saw the file, I recalled more details of the case. He had been a significant user of Dilaudid, an incredibly powerful painkiller with effects similar to those of heroin. The crime had been that he had been in illegal possession of this powerful prescription narcotic. Upon a presentence psychiatric evaluation, he had been found to have antisocial tendencies which made him a candidate for Atascadero. (As he later told me, "I was a schemer, and I couldn't see that a lot of my schemes were against the law.'')

When I reflected upon how effectively he ran that meeting, and what a model prisoner he had been, I resolved to do something helpful about Mr. Vasquez. I arranged for a probation hearing. Vasquez said that he was ready for probation, and that he wanted to become involved in the construction business.

I looked at him and told him that I would take a chance on him. "If you're really serious about a new life, I'll give you thirty days out of jail to make your new life. If you can get a job and start working within thirty days, I'll lengthen your probation and let you get on with your life.''

Vasquez and I also exchanged suggestions about getting into the construction business. I told him that I would call a few friends in the construction business and see what I could do for him. But despite the best efforts of longtime friends in construction, I could not help Vasquez get a job there. Those jobs for which he was qualified by skill were union jobs, especially in the stone mason area, where he was best. The unions in question would not accept people with criminal records as new members.

After a few weeks, when he still had no job, I spoke to Vasquez. "I'm scared," he said. "If I don't get a legitimate job, I'll go back to using and selling drugs. I don't want to do that. I want any kind of job at all that gives me a chance.''

I called a wonderful friend from my days at the University of Southern California, a fraternity brother and now a successful stationer, with a number of wholesale outlets. "Will you take a chance on someone I recommend?" I asked. "Even if he has a record?"

The ties of youth, especially if tended into middle age, are strong ties indeed. Again, maybe that was the mark of a different era, but we trusted each other and helped each other. Especially, he trusted my judgment. He hired Vasquez as a shipping clerk and loader of supplies. He never regretted it.

Within a year, Vasquez was head of my friend's shipping department. His salary had doubled, from $75 to $150 per week. He was far from rich, but he was making something of his life. I was gratified at my efforts in his behalf. It showed me that trust and helping still could achieve results. It showed me that when you believe in a man, you can put yourself behind him and not regret it. I have always believed that real human concern should take the form of hands-on helping, and my feelings were entirely vindicated by the success of Vasquez.

It got even better. After about another year, during which I had stayed in contact with Vasquez, he called me up to ask me if I would do him a favor.

"I've gotten engaged," he said. "She's a wonderful woman, divorced with two sons, and I want you to marry us."

I thought about it for a moment. "Have you told her everything about you?" I asked.

"Almost everything," he said.

"When you've told her everything, then let's talk about it," I answered.

A few days later, he called back. "I've told her about the drugs and about Atascadero," he said elatedly. "She still wants to marry me."

"I'll do it," I said, "and what's more, I'll do it in my home."

That was more than twenty years ago, but I remember every bit of it vividly. A tennis-playing friend, the famous actor Gilbert Roland, sent Vasquez four bottles of fine champagne. Our sons, who were twelve and thirteen, were the official photographers. It was a happy day. My wife and I gave the couple an electric can opener. Even though I did not realize it at the time, the gift probably had symbolic significance, since my trust in Vasquez was the "opener" that got him out from his own steel container.

Vasquez adopted his wife's two sons. One is now a daring Air Force pilot. The other is a lawyer. I was proud to send letters for one to the Air Force Academy and the other to Loyola Law School in Los Angeles. For the last ten years, Vasquez himself has had his own business building and installing decorative, custom-made fireplaces. I still talk to him often and exchange long letters. Several years ago, his wife had to go into the hospital for a rare kidney illness. She was put on a long waiting list at UCLA hospital, the premier facility in this area for kidney work. I explained to the doctors the gravity of her case and helped her get into the hospital earlier than scheduled.

(Normally, I would never use "connections" to put one woman ahead of another for entry to a hospital. But in Mrs. Vasquez' case, if she had not been admitted almost immediately, her very survival was in question.)

The Vasquez case is an example of what people can still do for each other, and of what society has to offer to its members. In a sense, everyone involved was satisfied. Society caught Vasquez in a crime and made him spend time in prison. But society, through a judge, also found the heart to give him another chance to live a useful life. He was only thirty years old when I saw him at Atascadero. He still had a long life to offer for the betterment of society and his family-to-be. Society's faith in him, through me, was completely justified.

In the case of Mr. Vasquez, the criminal justice system itself actually functioned as a sort of neighborhood. It punished a neighbor who had done wrong, but then it supported the neighbor and gave him an opportunity to give something back to the neighborhood.

I believe in law and order. But I also believe in human possibility, and I believe that to keep a potentially productive man in prison when he has learned his lesson and done his penance is just waste. Vasquez could have turned out to just be another drug dealer for the rest of a short life. But I had faith in what he could do if someone trusted him, and I was right. This, in every way, is the best kind of event I saw in criminal justice.

I did not stop taking chances with Vasquez.

About one year after my visit to Atascadero, I had before me the case of a man accused of robbing a bakery with a toy pistol. Now, under the law, it does not matter that the pistol was a toy. It is still capable of inspiring fear in the victims and of making them do what the man holding the gun wants them to do.

Accordingly, the man, whom I will call Billy Carpenter, was accused of armed robbery, which could carry a sentence of twenty years. Certainly, almost always, the accused, if convicted, spends time in a state penitentiary. But in Billy Carpenter's case, I found that such severity would have been an abuse of justice.

For one thing, Billy Carpenter and his family were starving. He was an unemployed electrician. More than that, he was a deeply confused young man, not able fully to pull his life together. He had a wife and a small son. The wife was severely ill and could not leave their small apartment. Billy Carpenter was at his wits' end. Second, when he had robbed the bakery, all he had taken was food. He had taken no money at all. He had taken bread to feed his wife and son.

Frankly, if I had imposed a lengthy state prison sentence on a man who was stealing bread with a toy pistol, I would not have been serving society or Billy Carpenter. I talked to him in court. He told me that since his incarceration, he had become a born-again Christian. He said that he now had a guiding force in his life. From what I saw, he had indeed acquired the self-discipline that might keep him out of trouble in the future. He gave the impression of being a changed man from the confused soul who had gone into the bakery with the toy pistol.

He pleaded guilty to the crime and I sentenced him to four months in the County Jail, a considerably less stringent place than any state penitentiary. I told him that following that time, he would be on probation. But if he was before me for a crime again, then he would surely do time, and a lot of it, at San Quentin or another state penitentiary.

As things turned out, Billy Carpenter did not shame me or himself. After he got out, he went to work as a full-time handyman at a large church in the suburbs of Los Angeles. Because he knew wiring and electricity, he was a valuable man for the pastor to have around. In time, he also became a lead male voice for the church choir. Every Christmas, he sends me a note and a record of his church choir singing Christmas songs. I listen to them and I feel glad that I took a chance.

Please understand that I do not conduct my cases in a Star Chamber. A case like Billy Carpenter's is highly visible. When I sentenced a man guilty of armed robbery to County Jail instead of the state penitentiary, I received a great deal of criticism for alleged leniency and coddling of criminals.

No one likes criticism, and that includes Joe Wapner. More important, since some of the criticism came from lawyers and public figures I respect, I had to take it seriously. But far more important is my own feeling for the man, the case, and the interests of society. Yes, I could feel the pain and the fear that must have been on the minds of men at the bakery whom Billy Carpenter robbed. They must have been terrified when what they thought was a real gun was pointed their way. All too many people die in those situations.

But I could also feel the pain of Billy Carpenter, and I could—and did—know in my gut that he would not be before me again charged with a crime if I and the society I represent gave him a chance.

If society is ever to become a feeling neighborhood again—a national imperative—we have to feel for everyone in the society, including those who have hurt society. To just say, "Throw the book at them," is a recipe for an unfeeling society which may function by some kind of casebook or statute book, but doesn't have the kind of human qualities that a working society must have.

In my courtroom, I dealt with human beings. The society I worked for and for whom I dispensed justice was made up of human beings. If I could not show feelings of compassion for a man who was starving, or a drug user who had real talent as a legitimate businessman, I would have just been a computer, and a rather primitive model at that, programmed to read a book and say what I read.

Pat Brown appointed me as a *man* to sit on the court. I passed judgment and imposed sentence as a *man* in a *community* on other *men* and *women*. I wanted to pull them back into the neighborhood. I often failed. But when I succeeded, it was a good day in court, and in that neighborhood which is all of us.

CHAPTER SIX

Imperfect Justice

*F*or most of man's history, when a person was accused of a crime, he was tried—if at all—by a magistrate or a policeman or a priest. That trier of the case could be an imperial prefect sent from Rome trying a Greek merchant or an Egyptian farmer. He could be a priest of one religion trying someone of another religion. The judge could simply be a friend of the king trying a case according to his whims or how he felt after lunch.

But in 1215, a great change took place in the world of law. An English king, the famous King John of the Robin Hood stories, was so cruel and oppressive to his subjects, especially to the noblemen of the realm, that they rose in revolt. Much of the king's army was away on the Crusades, and another group of the army was not inclined to fight and possibly die for King John. So the nobles had considerable leverage over the king. They could, and did, hold a peace treaty with him and required that he change his ways in a number of particulars if they were to lay down their arms.

One of the declarations they got from King John allowed Englishmen to feel secure in their homes during peacetime. Another set up a rudimentary beginning of Parliament. But the one that affects the legal system most crucially was trial by jury.

Because King John had an unfortunate habit of simply accusing nobles of treason, having a magistrate summarily find the accused guilty of treason, then seizing his land (and maybe his head), the nobles wanted a form of protection against such arbitrary "trials." The form that was demanded, and agreed to by a reluctant King John, was that from then on, nobles could not be tried for any serious crime except by a jury of their peers, or other noblemen.

From that precedent, set under the Magna Carta oak seven and a half centuries ago sprang the tree of trial by a jury of one's peers. While this is taken for granted in America and in the United Kingdom, it is a rare privilege, still unusual in the rest of the world.

Trial by jury is one of the greatest of all safeguards against the arbitrary authority of the government. As long as it takes the unanimous agreement of six or twelve men and women to put a man in jail or take away a woman's property, for example, the state cannot exercise uncontrolled power over life, freedom, or property. Trial by jury insists that ultimate legal power rests with the way the ordinary citizen interprets law and evidence—guided, of course, by a judge. (There can be trials in which the accused or civil litigants waive a jury trial and simply have the case tried before a judge. I will get to those cases—among my favorites—soon.)

But trial by jury has its pitfalls as well. Any system that relies upon human beings with different views on every subject from cars to God, and different abilities to understand even the basic facts of a case, inevitably involves severe, even heartbreaking, moments. Appreciation of the jury system often means accepting genuinely wrong out-comes of cases—at least as I saw them.

In 1962, a man whom I will call Steven Thorsten suspected his wife of having an affair with a man named "Carl Benson." Mr. Thorsten lived far out in the San Fernando Valley, almost to the Ventura County line. He was an accountant who worked in Thousand Oaks, then a small town just over the county line. His wife, who was about twenty-five, while he was fifty, worked as a payroll clerk at a seafood company in Manhattan Beach, almost forty miles from their home. Carl Benson owned the company. He was a handsome man in his thirties. Mr. Thorsten noticed, or thought he noticed, that his wife stayed unusually late at work, was uncommonly willing to work on Saturdays and Sundays, and came home smelling a lot more like perfume than like halibut.

Not only that, but sometimes at the company Christmas party and the company July 4 picnic, Mr. Thorsten thought he saw his wife holding hands with her boss. Finally, she got entirely too many personal calls at home from her boss. The calls started off with questions about ledger amounts but soon wound up with his wife giggling and blushing.

Like many couples in the same situation, Mr. and Mrs. Thorsten quarreled about allegations of affairs and infidel-ity. In fact, they quarreled often. One night, after our Mr. and Mrs. Thorsten had quarreled again, Mrs. Thorsten confessed: She had indeed been having a torrid affair with Carl Benson. She was sorry, but there it was.

Steven Thorsten was not happy. He thought for two days about the wrong that Carl Benson had done him. Then he decided to do something.

He took out his revolver. He taped it to the underside of

the hood over the engine of his Oldsmobile. Then he drove off to Manhattan Beach to see Carl Benson. He drove for forty miles. When he got to Benson's neighborhood he parked the car several blocks away, took out his revolver, hid it in his jacket, then walked to Benson's garage, and from across the street watched Benson cleaning a fish. (Apparently Benson had just returned from a sport fishing cruise off Coronado Beach, which was something of a busman's holiday, under the circumstances.) Benson was cleaning the fish with a fish *knife*.

Thorsten took the revolver out of its hiding place, held it in his hand, and strolled over to talk to Benson. A few minutes later, Benson was dead from a bullet wound. The bullet came from Thorsten's revolver, and Thorsten had pulled the trigger. After that, there was severe disagreement on almost every other fact of the case.

In particular, Mr. Thorsten said that he had carried the revolver with him just for protection while he engaged Carl Benson in a discussion of the rights and wrongs of seducing another man's wife. As Mr. Thorsten told it, Carl Benson attacked Thorsten with the fish knife. It was only by using the revolver he had so thoughtfully brought with him that Mr. Thorsten was able to defend himself. Clearly, according to Mr. Thorsten and his attorney, this was a case of self-defense.

The police and the prosecutor saw it differently. By their lights, a wronged husband had taken the trouble to conceal a revolver under the hood of an Oldsmobile. The same man had taken the trouble and time to drive across a large city with the revolver taped under his car hood. This was not the behavior of a man who does not intend to use that gun. If anything in the whole world involves premeditation—as the police and the prosecutor saw it—taping a revolver under your hood and driving forty miles to confront your wife's paramour does the trick.

The lawyer for the defense fought against the police version vigorously. In his closing summation, he strode back and forth in front of the jury box holding the sinister fish knife, waving it in front of the jurors' eyes, explaining how terrifying it would be to be attacked by a man carrying a fish knife.

To me, despite the excellent efforts of the defense lawyer, Thorsten was clearly guilty. I did not for a minute believe that he was carrying that gun in case Benson might be found cleaning a fish with a fish knife. How on earth would Thorsten even have known or had the slightest idea that Benson might be carrying a knife? If he had just wanted to have a conversation or warn away Benson, why didn't he telephone, or even go see him at work?

Still, the defense lawyer had scored his points with the jury. After two days of deliberations, they came back reporting that they were hopelessly deadlocked, eleven to one (but I was not allowed to ask in whose favor). In cases like this, I could have declared a mistrial immediately. But I was convinced that something drastically incorrect was taking place in the jury room. I sent the jurors back to reconsider. After another day they were still deadlocked, eleven to one. I sent them back another time. After another day, they were still deadlocked.

With the greatest possible reluctance, I had to discharge the jury as well as Steven Thorsten. In my mind, he had literally gotten away with murder.

Why did I not lecture the jury, explain to them the way I saw the case, and try to change the one holdout's mind?

Because in the American jury system, the judge is strictly charged with not attempting to persuade the jury. The jury decides on guilt or innocence. If I stepped in and used my knowledge of the law and my experienced way of seeing the facts and organizing them, it would have been Joe Wapner, and not twelve tried and true men and women who decided Thorsten's fate.

But do not let those high-sounding words fool you. I was extremely angry about the outcome of the Thorsten case. I, as a judge, had certain responsibilities under the law. I was required to restrain my passions and my temper. But the jurors had responsibilities as well. It was their job to be guided by the facts and the law, and not by their own prejudices, or by being scared by having a fish knife waved in their faces. The one woman who refused to see the facts clearly (at least as I saw them) and who allowed her mind to be made up on the basis of caprice had subverted what the jury system is all about. We trust juries because we believe they will not simply decide cases based on whims. When holdout jurors let killers go free because of a temporary moment of passion and sympathy, they discredit the whole jury system.

In that case, one might ask, should we throw the jury system away? Should we have cases, maybe capital cases only, tried before a judge and not a jury? Absolutely not. The jury system is not perfect. But it is still a major protector of our rights as Americans. If we junked it, we would not find another system as good. Besides, we cannot just start throwing out everything in the society that is not completely perfect. In a society of imperfect beings, their creations will not be perfect either. This will range from cars and washing machines to systems of trial. We just have to go with the method that works the best in terms of sometimes conflicting goals of the justice system: adjudging cases quickly and correctly on one hand, while making absolutely certain that the rights of the accused are guarded. Neither goal can take precedence over the other without our losing something invaluable.

So trial by jury coexists uneasily with perfect justice as the judge sometimes sees it, and sometimes the judge must swallow his fury at one particular outcome and remember that the system of trial by one's peers is still the best possible way of hearing a conflict where a man's life and liberty are at stake.

This is true even when you get cases like *The People of the State of California* v. *"Plato Smith."*

"Plato Smith" was a diminutive fellow who had a record of petty crimes. He lived in a small apartment building in South Central Los Angeles, not far from the campus of the University of Southern California, where I went to college and law school.

Mr. Smith lived with a woman who also had a record of petty crimes like shoplifting. One day, the couple apparently quarreled, as couples will do. The manager of the apartment was too scared to open her door and look out. Instead, she opened her peephole in her door and looked down the hall. As she later told it, she saw Plato Smith choking his friend while the woman struggled for life. Then she saw Plato Smith standing over the body, and then Plato Smith was gone.

Mr. Smith absolutely denied that he had done anything to the woman. Indeed, he said he was heartbroken to learn that she was dead. As to the eyewitness, he said she must have been mistaken. He was passed out drunk in his apartment waiting for the woman he loved to come home. He heard no struggle and first learned of the death when the police appeared at his door to arrest him, or so he said.

At the trial, the manager testified, and the police testified, and the medical examiner also testified. To my eyes, as judge in the case, the matter was absolutely clear cut. After all, how much more do you need than an impartial eyewitness who saw the crime in progress?

The case went to the jury. The jury deliberated for a surprisingly long time. After three days, they returned to my court. "We are hopelessly deadlocked," the foreman said.

I was stunned. "How do you stand numerically?" I asked. "Don't tell me whether it's for guilt or innocence."

"Eleven to one," said the foreman.

While I was collecting my thoughts, trying to decide what to do, whether to send the jury back for further deliberations or discharge them, I saw that the jurors were talking among themselves. "How would it be if we were allowed to go to the scene of the crime?" the foreman asked. "It might be that if we could see the scene and especially see how much you can see through the peephole, we might very well be able to reach a verdict."

I was delighted. The real scene, the actual locus of the crime, might well do the trick. In any event, I always believe that real life should be as much a part of a case as possible. The more a jury knows, the more likely it is to reach a sound verdict.

We made a journey, a judicial field trip, to the scene of the killing. The prosecutors, the defense lawyer, the bailiffs, the defendant, the jury, the court reporter, and I all went to the sad apartment house in South Central Los Angeles where Plato Smith had lived before he started living in County Jail.

The court reporter set up her machine. We started the proceedings in the apartment of the manager who had said she saw the crime. In turn, each juror, then everyone else, including me, looked through the peephole.

Now, as it happened, "peephole" was not the right name for this particular aperture. This was not a narrow little hole such as you might look through into a child's telescope. This was not an optical device that gives the viewer a fisheye look into a distorted hallway. The "peephole" was a large, unobstructed hole in the door, perhaps six inches by nine inches. One could see almost as well through that door as if the door were not there at all.

I brought the court and its participants back downtown and reassembled the jury in the jury room. After a few hours, the jury foreman again said he had an announcement. To my amazement, once again, the jury was deadlocked. The vote was still eleven to one, but that one juror would simply not change his vote.

This time I was deeply frustrated. I had to look at my daily written admonition to myself which I kept on my desk every day. It reads simply "Patience and Restraint." I was tempted to harangue the jury and persuade them to come to a unanimous verdict, one way or the other. But I restrained myself and simply sent them back for further deliberation.

But that one juror would not change his mind. After another day, I reluctantly declared a mistrial. When the jury was discharged, both the prosecutor and the defense attorney asked the jurors how the voting had gone. They soon learned that it had been eleven to one for conviction. At that point both sides were willing to plead guilty to second-degree murder. That way, the defense attorney's client would not face the consequences of first-degree murder if the case were retried. Grudgingly, I accepted the defendant's plea. I read a lengthy probation report on him, then gave him the maximum possible sentence for second-degree murder. To me, he was still getting off too easily.

I tell this story—and the story of the Thorsten case—to illustrate that even the best institutions of the law are far from perfect. But I also tell them to point out that every human being in society, at least in a society of laws, must compromise. A citizen might get the impression that judges, sitting on the bench, ordering people around, deciding cases, must surely be beyond the need to compromise. Fortunately, that is not so. Even a judge must behave strictly in accordance with the law. He is as restrained by the law as anyone else. Yes, I would have loved to insist on my view of the cases of Thorsten and Smith. That would have been my inclination as a man, to insist on getting the case settled my way. But as a judge, I was under the law, just as any other American.

Under the famous oak at Runnymede, where King John signed the Magna Carta, a system of judging human beings so as to protect them against arbitrary authority was born. Under that tree, the whole idea of law as restrained and measured by some standard other than one man's wishes was planted. The price we pay for the growth of that idea is that judges who know—at least we think we know—how a case should turn out are prevented from imposing our arbitrary authority in a case even if the result is that a guilty man—as we see him—goes free or gets off too lightly. To my way of thinking, that is an acceptable price. But make no mistake, it is a price. The system metes out justice, but no one should consider it perfect.

Not yet, and probably not ever.

CHAPTER SEVEN

Jurisprudential Delinquents

*B*ut then there is the case of Vernon Cleveland . . . .
Mr. Cleveland, Esquire and Gentleman, practiced criminal law in Los Angeles. When I had been on the bench for two years in Superior Court, his face had become quite familiar to me. He handled many different cases simultaneously, and he always gave the impression of a juggler tossing case jackets into the air and hoping that he could somehow keep them from falling.

He couldn't do it.

Even though he was a former deputy attorney general and a lawyer of ten years' experience, he was chronically late for cases. Often he simply did not appear, or appeared so late that he made it impossible to address his case that day. Throughout the Criminal Department of Superior Court, he was notorious for his habitual lateness, and that is not a good reason to be known.

One day in April of 1964, Vernon Cleveland had two cases pending before me in Department 100 of the Superior Court. As it happened, Mr. Cleveland had been so incautious as to have two other cases pending in other departments of the Superior Court. One of them was a jury returning to give a verdict in a criminal case in which his client was the defendant.

Cleveland completed his attention to one of the cases before me. Then, during a brief recess, he was told that he had to go to another room to hear the jury's verdict. Therefore, when I resumed court, handling a very busy Master Calendar, where all criminal cases are assigned, Mr. Cleveland was gone. I had already suffered for two years with his relentless lateness. I was annoyed for myself and for the rest of the people in court. Because he was absent, the judge, the bailiffs, the other lawyers—even Mr. Cleveland's client— had to twiddle their thumbs while we wondered where he was. After a few minutes, I sent my bailiff out into the hallway to find Mr. Cleveland and bring him back.

Incredibly, Mr. Cleveland did not return to my courtroom. Later, he told the schoolboy's story that he thought my bailiff was from another courtroom and he got lost going to that courtroom! (It reminded me very much of students claiming that they actually completed their homework but somehow it had inexplicably gotten lost on the school bus. Or perhaps their dogs had chewed it up! Interestingly enough, even though Mr. Cleveland "thought" he was supposed to go to another courtroom and not mine, he somehow never showed up in that courtroom either.)

When the bailiff came back and told me that Mr. Cleveland refused to return to the courtroom where his client was sitting accused of a felony, I was deeply concerned. Here was a lawyer, sworn to the highest duty of care for his clients, simply refusing the order of a judge, empowered by the laws of California, to return to defend his client.

In a very swift hurry, I sent my bailiff back out to the court to fetch Mr. Cleveland and to arrest him if necessary. This time, the bailiff could not even find Mr. Cleveland.

I was steaming. Now, in my public as well as my private life, I do not ask for any special treatment. I do not make headwaiters give me special tables in restaurants, and I always wait in line with everybody else. Without my robes on, I am just the same as any other Joe. But in my court, I represent the law.

I saw incredibly fine men, with families and children waiting for them back home, men with the fullest possible measure of decency and courage, get blown to pieces by Japanese artillery to preserve our system of law. When I came back from Cebu, I had to call wives and mothers and tell them that their sons were not coming back alive, and I knew then they had died to keep us all under a system of law. When I sat in Department 100 and thought of a *lawyer* thumbing his nose at the law, I became truly determined to set an example.

I immediately cited Mr. Cleveland for contempt. Now, it pains me to say that this lawyer's record for contemptuous behavior was so bad that I had already been forced to cite him for contempt and impose a small fine once before. Now, I was done with fines. I ordered Mr. Cleveland found and put in County Jail for two days.

You can probably imagine that lawyers are all too accustomed to seeing anybody but themselves in jail. When Mr. Cleveland learned that he, a member of the bar, was going to be put in jail, like the men and women he represented, he was hysterically upset. In fact, he at first thought I was joking. I was not.

Mr. Cleveland was not lazy. He appealed his jail term immediately, and he raised some ingenious defenses.

Mainly, he said that he could not be summarily sentenced for contempt because he had not been there in person! To me, this was the precise equivalent of a child who murders his parents then pleads for mercy from the court because he is an orphan.

The Supreme Court of California heard Mr. Cleveland's arguments and weighed them carefully. Then the high court of California affirmed my sentence of contempt. Their reasoning was beautiful. The opinion by Justice Stanley Mosk was so clearly set out, and makes the problems of running a court so clear, that I would like to quote a few lines from it:

"When an attorney fails to appear in court with his client, particularly in a criminal matter, the wheels of justice must temporarily grind to a halt. The client cannot be penalized, nor can the court proceed in the absence of counsel. Having allocated time for this case, the court is seldom able to substitute other matters. Thus the entire administration of justice falters. . . .

"In the case before us, we cannot find [Cleveland's] conduct to have been excusable. While it may be true that he could not avoid the conflict, he did little to mitigate the effects of the proceedings before Judge Wapner. His client was left unrepresented and the court lost precious time that vanished forever. . . ."

It is rare that a reader gets to see poetry in an appellate court opinion. Appreciation is in order, especially by the judge whose opinion was upheld.

Word of Mr. Cleveland's fate spread around the Superior Court. For over a year, lawyers were scrupulously on time. Then old habits came back. They came back particularly viciously for a lawyer whom I will call "Tom Shearing." Not to put too fine a point on it, Mr. Shearing was a scandalous liar. When he said something in court, I simply had no idea at all about whether it was true. I would probably have been well-advised to assume that whatever he told me was not true. I had endured five years, off and on, of his phony claims that clients were ill or unavoidably out of town or that he had not filed a brief because he had to do National Guard service.

In addition, he had the terrible habit of doing something harmful, drinking or drugs or whatever, which rendered him late and extremely *vague* (to be kind about it) after lunch.

One day a client of Mr. Shearing's was on trial for grand theft auto. The trial went fairly smoothly in the morning and then we recessed for lunch. When we reassembled after lunch, there was one prominent absentee from my court. Mr. Shearing was not there. I sent my bailiff out to find him, without success. He was simply not in the courthouse.

After about half an hour, into my courtroom came waltzing Attorney Shearing. He made as if to slip invisibly into his seat, as if no one would have noticed that the defense attorney in a criminal trial were missing!

"Where have you been, Counselor?" I asked him. "What's your excuse?"

"I suddenly remembered at lunch that I had a doctor's appointment for severe headaches that have been bothering me," he said.

"All right," I asked. "What's your doctor's name and phone number?"

Surprisingly, Mr. Shearing blurted them both out. Then

the race began. I bolted for my chambers to my phone. Simultaneously, Mr. Shearing ran for the pay phones in the hallway.

I knew that playing tennis and not smoking for all those years would pay off some day and it did. I reached Mr. Shearing's doctor while he was still panting and patting his pockets for change in the hallway. The doctor came right on the line, and in an appropriately respectful, apologetic tone, he told me that Mr. Shearing was indeed a patient, but had not been in for several months.

I returned to the courtroom to face an unrepentant Mr. Shearing. "It was another doctor," he said when I told him the results of my investigation. "I gave you the wrong name."

"You certainly did something wrong," I said. "That'll be fifty dollars for contempt, and you're getting off dirt cheap."

I brought down my gavel, and Mr. Shearing meandered away. I wish I could say that Mr. Shearing mended his ways and then went on to become a model member of the bar. I am sorry to say that he did not. Sadly, he made legal history a few years later for his brazen dishonesty in court.

He was called upon to be in court, fully prepared, for a criminal case in the Court in Los Angeles. He failed to show up, leaving his client stranded.

When he was called before the Court, he told the judge that he had suddenly and urgently been summoned to defend clients in a major national security case before a federal court in Ohio. In fact, as was revealed by a cursory investigation, he had never been involved in the case he discussed, and—more to the point—there was no such case as the one he described. For this, he was sentenced to jail for contempt. He appealed, astoundingly enough, but the Appeals Courts was as unimpressed as I had been. As far as I know, he served his brief penance in jail, and is now back to work as a lawyer.

I suspect that he learned very little from his brush with me in terms of honesty. He did learn, however, that I can run to the telephone faster than he can.

"Patience and Restraint" reads the motto on my desk. Maintain a judicial temperament, I remind myself. That's the goal. But for lawyers who mock the law, mock the blood that it has cost to keep us under law, waste everyone else's time, and desert their clients, I have a better slogan: "Throw the book at 'em."

CHAPTER EIGHT

And Throw Away the Key

*F*or a young woman from Salisbury, Maryland, Susan R. was doing very well in the summer of 1965. She had come out to Los Angeles one year before to study drama at UCLA. She had been the first woman in the history of Salisbury State College to go to graduate school in drama anywhere, let alone in the motion-picture capital of the world, Los Angeles. She was also the first woman in her family, all of whom were oystermen on the Chesapeake Bay, to attend graduate school of any kind, or even to finish college. She had already played Portia in a student production of *The Merchant of Venice*, updated and set in Los Angeles, with modern sets and costumes. With her clear, high voice and her coppery-auburn straight hair down to her shoulders, and her green eyes, she had every reason to think that her life had nowhere to go but up.

In Los Angeles, while it is almost never cool during the afternoon, the nights can on rare occasions get down to the forties or even the high thirties, sometimes even in the spring. That was a facet of Los Angeles life which Susan R. had difficulty adjusting to. She missed the balmy, warm nights in Salisbury, when she could sleep with the windows open, and hear the wind whistling through the marsh and the crickets hovering over the dock, and see the fireflies playing in the night air over the creek and the bay.

In July of 1965, by what seemed to Susan R. like a stroke of nostalgic luck, a week of Santa Ana winds blew over Los Angeles. These hot, dry winds glide across the deserts of Utah and Nevada, are heated by the sun, then sucked into the moist expanse of the Pacific Ocean. They put the whole city on edge, for reasons not fully known. Perhaps they were meant to blow against sand and cactus and not against a metropolitan area of ten million already edgy men, women, and children.

Susan R. welcomed the winds because they and they alone made Los Angeles warm at night. For the first five nights of the Santa Anas, she left her windows open in her apartment on Veteran Avenue in Westwood, just across from the sprawling Veterans Cemetery. She could not hear any crickets, but she could hear the sound of the nearby ten-lane San Diego Freeway. Its endless whoosh was almost like the sound of the water during a storm. She had no roommates to complain about the safety hazard of leaving her windows open, which was just as well, because she was completely determined to have some real air, even hot smoggy air, instead of air-conditioned air for just one week.

On the sixth night of the Santa Ana week, Susan R. again left her windows open, with the hot air leaking through the screens. She fell asleep in her underwear while studying lines of *Death of a Salesman*. Perhaps the sound of the traffic helped her to sleep.

She awakened at about 3 A.M. and knew, the way humans know, that someone was in her room. As soon as she opened her eyes, she saw a man with a stocking over his face and a straight razor in his hand. The man put a rough, oily-smelling other hand over Susan R's face. "Just be quiet," he said. "I'm not gonna hurt you. I only want to take whatever money you have. Just show me where your money is, and I'll leave."

Susan R. was far too smart even to think about dying for money. She nodded agreement, and pointed at her bureau drawer where she kept her purse. The intruder pulled her over to the purse and made her take all the money, less than twenty dollars, out of the purse and give it to him.

The man was angry that there was so little money. "What else do you have?" he asked.

Susan R. took him to her bedside table. She gave him a pair of pearl earrings. "This is it," she said. "Unless you want my Volkswagen keys."

The man looked at the pearls, looked at Susan, and slapped her across the face. "I want a lot more than that," he said. He ripped off her underpants, slit the back of her brassiere with his razor, and then told her to have oral sex with him. When she resisted, he punched her in the face and told her that the next time he would cut her throat.

She orally copulated the intruder. Then he asked her if she had any beer in the house. She gave him a beer and begged him to leave. He told her that he was lonely and wanted to talk to her. "If you get to know me," he said, "I think you'll like me."

Susan became hysterical. She started to beg and cry for him to leave. When he went to the toilet, he dragged her with him to make sure she did not call the police. When she told him that she had a boyfriend coming over, he slapped her across the face yet again. Then he forced her to have sexual intercourse with him, while holding a razor against her throat.

After he had been there for two hours, he used her telephone to call two friends (!) to have them come over. "I think I'll share you with them," he said. A few moments later, there was the shriek of a police siren outside the apartment house. The assailant panicked. He bolted for the window. In the process, because he forgot he was dragging Susan around by her wrist, he slashed her cheek with his razor. Her blood flew all over the room, including onto his clothes. Then he let go of her and left.

Susan was in UCLA's emergency room for the rest of the night. She did not leave until almost noon, what with her interviews with the police and doctors. Then she realized that the intruder had told his friends where she lived. She would not go to her apartment at all. She stayed for a week at a friend's home in Sherman Oaks. For all that time, she could not sleep. After a week of insomnia and delayed stress shock, she had to be admitted to the UCLA Psychiatric Ward for severe anxiety states.

After that, she went back to Salisbury. She only returned for the trial of Homer Lee, who was caught by the telephone number he had dialed in his access of generosity, as well as by the bloodstain on his shirt. The brutalization of Susan R. was not by any means his first sex offense, and in fact he had a record for sexual abuses of various kinds stretching back to his days in juvenile court, almost ten years before. He had not done what he did by accident.

Let me tell you my feelings about rape. Despite a few exceptions, forcible rape is carried on almost exclusively by men against women. It is a repulsive crime of violence against one sex alone, for all practical purposes. It is no longer a rare occurrence, if it ever was. In a city the size of Los Angeles, about three thousand rapes are reported to the LAPD and the sheriff each year. People in a position to know believe that there may well be ten times that many which go unreported.

Every woman, from studio executive to manicurist to homeless person, knows someone who has been raped, usually brutally. All of this means that for women, and only for women, there is a permanent climate of fear of being raped. The fear may be more or less immediate, but it is always there. Every woman who is thinking about a dark street or a door without a good lock or a walk to her car in the parking lot must think as well about the possibility of rape.

In a way, it is as if a war were being waged against one sex by certain violent members of the other sex. Or, looked at another way, women in any city are always in a state of fear like that brought on by repeated, endless terrorism. Rape is a form of random, but very deadly, terrorism against women. I have seen the effects in women's faces, in their lives, and the lives of those around them. Rape is a physical and psychological barrage against women.

There are those who have suggested that rape is a sort of conspiracy by all men against all women. To me, this is simply not true. As a judge and as a man, I can say conclusively that the ordinary man never commits rape, never even thinks about committing rape, and is horrified and revolted by those men who do rape.

Further, not all rapes are the same. There are violent, almost unimaginably cruel rapes, far worse than the one that Homer Lee inflicted on Susan R. There are also date rapes in which it is difficult indeed to tell where the foreplay stopped and where the compulsion began. There are also, sad to say, many reported rapes that simply did not happen. But even if we take the most obvious, incontrovertible facts about rapes, there are entirely too many of them, and they inexcusably put innocent women into a state of terror. When I hear laymen snickering that victims "asked for it," I feel disgusted. Women do not "ask" to be raped any more than men ask to be murdered.

All of this has come through my mind in the dozens of rape cases I have heard. By the time I left the Superior Court, my feelings about rapes were well known. It was a foolish lawyer who argued a rape case for the defense in my court and expected to prevail.

The public defender in the case of Homer Lee had no choice. She was simply assigned to me on the Master Calendar. To be fair, I can think of no judges in Los Angeles known to be easy on rapists, so she—the woman public defender—simply took her best shot with me.

She pleaded that Homer Lee should be looked upon as in need of treatment rather than punishment because, she said at pretrial, he was insane and not responsible for his acts. She asked that he be sent to Atascadero where, she insisted, he would soon be rehabilitated and made into a productive member of society.

To start with, the insanity defense is a can of worms in almost every situation. If a defense lawyer is sufficiently energetic, he or she can almost always find two psychiatrists to say that a defendant is schizophrenic or cannot deal with reality or is hallucinating during the hours of midnight to seven A.M. every day. Then the prosecution can always find two more psychiatrists to say that the defendant is as normal as Mom and apple pie.

That turns legal cases about facts and law into medical

conventions. The jury inevitably gets confused and finds that it is grasping to understand a great deal of psychiatric jargon. In the final analysis, the facts of a case are often left gasping in the dust.

To make matters worse, once one starts thinking about the insanity defense, it is hard to know where to stop. For example, if a man has committed a brutal murder, his defense lawyer and a learned psychiatrist may say that he had to have been insane to have done such a terrible thing. After all, they will say, what sane person will put a victim in a car trunk and shoot a shotgun into it? That argument makes a great deal of sense.

But if everyone who commits a violent crime is insane by definition, then we are left in the impossible position of saying that the act of committing a violent crime is itself the excuse for not being prosecuted for the crime.

That would mean that defendants would automatically get off with an insanity plea just for having committed a violent crime! That would completely avoid the need of society to punish crime or even to define acts as crimes.

On the other hand, clearly some people are more capable of premeditation than others. To hold a babbling street derelict who punches someone as guilty as a man who schemes to punch someone at his office, or to think that a man who really did hear angelic voices telling him to burn down his house is as guilty as a man who did it for the insurance might also be unrealistic and unjust.

But in the case of Susan R., I did not need to reach such complex issues. Her pain was so tangible in her tormented, but still pretty face, in the gash on her cheek, in the trembling hands she could barely keep still, that I did not need to reach for subtleties.

"This man has done a terrible, traumatic act if indeed he is guilty of the crimes with which he is charged," I said. "As a judge representing the needs of society, I am simply not free to allow him to plead insanity, to possibly go to Atascadero, then possibly be released when he says he has come to his senses. That option does not take into account the overwhelming need of society to be protected from men who commit brutal rapes, the need of victims like Miss R. to feel free to sleep at night knowing that her assailant, whoever he might be, is behind bars, and the imperative need for people who commit this kind of crime to be punished severely."

At trial, Homer Lee raised a number of interesting and even ingenious defenses through his capable woman defense attorney. He protested in particular that blood tests should not be allowed in rape cases because they were too vague and could not definitely prove that he was the rapist. But I ruled that a blood test could be used to show that a defendant could not be completely excluded as the possible assailant, with sufficiently clear instructions to the jury.

The jury found Homer Lee guilty as charged. I gave him the maximum sentence under the law. When I last looked, he was still in state penitentiary, which is a good place for him. I have no doubt that there was at least a hint of merit in his public defender's claims that he was mentally ill. But in a case like his, sessions on the analyst's couch are not the answer. As long as he is severely dangerous, punishment and detention are the only ways to protect society, to make sure that he does not do it again, to deter him and others, and to ensure that Miss R., who only wanted to be in the theater, can have even a slender thread of justice. We all hope for rehabilitation of offenders and sometimes it happens. But the first need of society is for protection of the innocent.

Again, the public defender was not wrong to do what she did. Her job is to try every avenue to get her client freed. That is our system of law, and it's a damned good one. But the maneuverings of a brilliant lawyer and the reams of material on the insanity defense did not outweigh a basic fact: He had done a terrible wrong to an innocent woman. Society had to make him pay.

A dash of common sense was called for about eight years later in another bizarre case involving rape. On Ventura Boulevard in the San Fernando Valley, in Sherman Oaks, there are several rather pleasant piano bars. As a judge, I was always too busy to spend time in bars, but I had passed by them, and they always looked cheerful and harmless.

They were not quite as harmless as they seemed. For several months in 1973, a man had gone into a series of these bars, met women, persuaded them to let him drive them home, then taken them up into the hills of Los Angeles and forcibly raped them. To add another note of danger, he had then left them there, often without clothes, in the rough, frightening brush of Los Angeles, far from any kind of help. When a victim stumbled back to a road where she might be helped, she did not know if the man in the car might be yet another danger.

Once, the rapist was in such a good mood after his crime that he took the victim home and dropped her off at her house in Van Nuys. This was his big mistake. He was caught through his license number soon thereafter. At trial, his lawyer waived a jury, which surprised me a great deal. Usually in rape cases, the defense lawyer wants a jury trial.

He wants at least a chance of getting an angry housewife or a slightly disturbed mechanic who somehow can be made to believe that the complaining witness was "asking for it," to reuse that horrible phrase.

I accepted the jury waiver happily. As you can probably tell by now, I prefer trying cases by myself, even as I realize the indispensable nature of the jury system. No sooner had I opened the trial than defense counsel asked if he and his client could see me in chambers. They came into my chambers along with the prosecutor and defense counsel and made the unusual request that the defendant be allowed to take down his trousers and show me his penis.

"Is this necessary for the defense?" I asked.

"Yes, Your Honor, it is," said the defense counsel solemnly.

The defendant took down his pants. In a gingerly way, the defense counsel pointed out that defendant had on his penis a large growth, like a wart only much larger. Then the defendant covered himself.

"What is the relevance of this?" I asked.

"Your Honor," said defense counsel, "the relevance is that because of defendant's unusual anatomy, it would be impossible, we submit, for defendant to have had sex with any of the complaining witnesses without their commenting on an unusual aspect of that sex, namely defendant's growth on his male sex organ."

The defense counsel, a man with a patch over one eye like in the old Hathaway shirt advertisements, said it all quite seriously. But I did not entertain even the slightest thought of granting the ensuing motion for dismissal.

"You have got to be kidding," I said. "A woman is taken up to the hills at night. She is brutally raped by force and in fear for her life. A woman in that set of circumstances is hardly likely to spend a lot of time and attention noticing if the defendant's penis might or might not have a growth. Common sense tells the court that you are presupposing a calm, extremely sensitive, and even clinical approach at a time when a woman would feel nothing but fear and shock. Let's get back to court.''

By the way, I found defendant guilty.

CHAPTER NINE

Beetlemania

*T*hen there is the occasional bug in the criminal justice system.

In 1960, when I was on the Municipal Court, a woman appeared before me virtually staggering under the weight of her diamond and emerald jewelry. She was from a well-known family of land barons in Beverly Hills, and her picture often peered out at me from the society pages of the newspapers.

Mrs. Van Peel, as I will call her, was charged with driving erratically on Santa Monica Boulevard, including driving on the shoulder and weaving in and out of traffic by using the shoulder.

"How do you plead?" I asked her.

"Not guilty," she said forthrightly.

"Do you deny that you were driving on the shoulder?"

"Not at all," she said.

"Then how do you believe you are not guilty?"

"Your Honor," she said, "I was driving the maid's car. My Cadillac was getting a tune-up. I know that if I drove a Cadillac on the shoulder, that would be a no-no. But I was just driving a Volkswagen bug,'' she said. "Surely that's not counted as a real car."

"Yes, it is counted as a real car," I said. "And I'm fining you a real fifty dollars, and leaving this building without paying is a no-no."

I never saw her in court again.

CHAPTER TEN

Under the Robes

A judge is first and foremost a human being. He succeeds or fails in his work to the extent that he can feel for the men and women before him, and then integrate those feelings into the context of the legal system. A judge is a man (or a woman, of course) when he is hearing evidence, studying precedents, examining documents, or hearing oral arguments. His humanity is at issue in every act from the bench.

A judge is also a man when he is writing a book. There are bills to be paid, clothes to be cleaned, new people to meet, old friends to take to dinner. These present facts of life throw into relief and illustrate to me what is important about the past. That is, what is happening to me today, as I write this, tells me a great deal about what counts and what does not in the past. The events of this morning or this afternoon shape my understanding of where the human connection was in all of the cases of my past.

I am now going to take you behind the scenes of this particular judge's life, so to speak, and share with you the most wonderful possible experience of the present that could touch a judge's life or a writer's life. Just as I started writing this chapter, my son David and his wife Edna had a baby son, Ariel. They already have a wonderful son, Gabriel, so Ariel is the second grandchild for my wife Mickey and me.

As I looked at Ariel in his crib and in his mother's and father's arms, I thought about the beginning of life and where life leads. Like any grandfather, I thought about how far I have come from when I was a baby and my grandparents were looking at me. The trip has taken sixty-seven years so far, and is still exciting every single day. But I think that in order for you to understand why some things mean so much to me, it might help to understand a few facts of the early part of that voyage. They help me, at any rate, to understand the landmarks along the way. They help to understand who I am, not just as a judge but as the human being inside the robes.

I was born in Los Angeles in the year after the end of World War I. It was then a metropolitan area of fewer than one million souls, contrasted with its present population of over twelve million. My father was a lawyer. He had originally planned to be a doctor, but could not afford to study medicine full time, which was the only way it was offered then and now. Law school, however, was offered at night. He could therefore work during the day to support himself while he studied. He was the kind of lawyer whom you used to see on television shows: he worked out of a small office downtown. He was not part of a huge law department of a mammoth corporation or part of a multicity law firm as many lawyers are today. He worked by himself, and was the researcher, investigator, and attorney on every one of his cases, and worked tirelessly, even when he was exhausted.

I grew up in middle-class circumstances in what is now almost downtown Los Angeles. My parents lived in a duplex with my grandparents. Every day when I came home from school, I would run up the stairs to my grandparents' home and talk with them and my aunt for hours. From my earliest recollections, they took me seriously, and listened— and talked—to me as if I were an adult. That means a great deal to the self-esteem of a child.

If I have grown to be a man with a concern for other people, as a judge must be, much of it was learned from my grand-parents and my aunt. My grandmother was deeply concerned with helping those in dire straits. She was, through most of my childhood, head of a local ladies' aid society. If I have a sense of humor, which a judge must have if he is to survive, I learned it largely from my grandfather, a man of wit on every subject. My connectedness with the larger world came largely from my aunt Esther. From her (she was only twelve years older than I was) I learned how to dance, how to drive a car, and even how to pick out clothes that looked decent on me. Today's young people often live hundreds and even thousands of miles from grandparents, aunts, and uncles. Perhaps they believe they are well off, liberated in some way because of that distance. Maybe they are. For me, having an extended family was a rich gift every day. That gift has shaped me in ways that today's children may never even know, giving me adult counsel and examples of adult be-havior beyond my immediate family, and thereby giving me room to grow into a more comfortable pattern of adulthood. It has been fifty or more years since I used to burst into their home and start talking about what had happened that day, and I still miss my grandparents keenly.

My father worked extremely hard, as I said. He would

come home at the end of the day drained from struggling in court and in the library for his clients. I recall night after night when he would give us a slightly delayed replay of his fights in court on behalf of the little guy—always the little guy—who was being done out of an insurance settlement by a big company, or had his utilities unjustly shut off, or who had not been paid for goods delivered to a huge chain of dry-goods stores.

To my childish eyes, it seemed as if my father were fighting against giants every hour of every day, and always giving as good as he got. I sometimes went to see him in court. He could give a stem-winder of a jury summation that would make even bailiffs cry.

His passion, his strength, his whole life, seemed to me to be bent on preserving the rights and the livelihood of small people caught in a huge, impersonal system they barely understood. He did not always win by any means. But he never quit.

My mother was the kind of housewife you used to see in advertisements for refrigerators. She really did put a clean house and a hot dinner for her children and her husband above every other consideration. My father would have to fight against an extremely uncooperative world in court, but at home, his dinner was always on the table exactly when he wanted it to be.

Please do not misunderstand the childhood of Joe Wapner. I was not the third son in "Ozzie and Harriet." My father was and is a strong-willed, domineering, argumentative man. My grandparents and I were also strong-willed and argumentative. The result was a number of spirited "discussions" about almost every aspect of family life.

In one loud cacophony there would be complaints about "Dirty Collar Collins," a lawyer who had just pulled a fast one in court, questions about why my bat and ball happened to be in the middle of the walk to the front door, inquiries about why my homework was not getting done, and then rebuttals to all of the foregoing matters.

When I went from junior high school to high school, I wanted to be an actor. Through a friend of my father, I was allowed to transfer from my neighborhood high school to the famed Hollywood High School. Hollywood High had a reputation of having the best drama program in town. Even then, child stars including Marge Champion, Nanette Fabray and others, were pouring out of it.

In my senior year, after dozens of unsuccessful tryouts, I finally got a part in the senior class play. By coincidence—at the time I thought it was a prophetic coincidence—I was to play a man called Tallant in a play entitled *The Late Christopher Bean*. I rehearsed and practiced and read my lines in front of the mirror. Little by little, I convinced myself that I must be pretty damned good at it. In fact, I thought I must be a pretty hot item altogether.

One day, as I walked down the hall at Hollywood High with a friend, I saw an amazingly beautiful auburn-haired girl talking to virtually the whole football team. She was certainly the most attractive girl I had ever seen at Hollywood High or anywhere else until that time. My friend said that he could introduce me, and he did. I made small talk with her and then asked her if she would go for a soda after school. To my amazement, she said she would.

We went to a nearby drugstore and had Cokes. After we drank them, I realized that I had no money at all with me, not even enough to buy a Coke. Judy Turner gracefully paid for them. She was so graceful and cheerful that I invited her to a Saturday-night dance at Hollywood High. Again, to my delight, she agreed to go.

Judy Turner looked ravishing at the dance in a black velvet dress. I still recall picking her up at her mother's house north of Hollywood Boulevard near the Hollywood Bowl. I remember my pride that I—soon to be a major star, surely—walked into the dance with the prettiest girl in the room on my arm.

Alas, at the dance Judy Turner had other interests besides me. We did the fox-trot and at every step I could sense her looking over my shoulder to see who was more important or richer or better-looking. Judy Turner was gorgeous, but she was also a little bit more of a politician than I was used to.

Still, I took her home and kissed her good night and anticipated a bright future with her once I had taught her that I was the only young man worth looking at.

The very next day, when I was rehearsing in a special session as Mr. Tallant, the drama coach, Mr. Kachel, took me aside. In a direct way, he told me that I was simply not talented enough to play Mr. Tallant. I was out of the senior class play on my ear.

Not only that, but the next time I asked out Judy Turner, I was turned down flat. And the time after that. I was out of the running for stardom and out of the running for Judy Turner in one week.

Like everyone else in my family, I was competitive indeed and no quitter. Despite Mr. Kachel's obviously confused view of my abilities onstage, I decided that after high school I would go to Los Angeles City College. LACC was reputed to have the best drama classes in town at the college level. Moreover, it would allow me the scheduling leeway actually to work as an actor while I took my drama classes. As far as I could see, it was still ordained—Mr. Kachel or not—that I was to be the next Tyrone Power.

My strong-willed father had other ideas. He "urged" me strongly to go to the University of Southern California instead of studying acting. After much earnest debate, and only to humor him—because I had by then actually been told that I *looked like* Tyrone Power—I enrolled at USC. My erstwhile date and girlfriend Judy Turner was more determined about her acting. She continued to study drama, dyed her hair blond, changed her name to Lana, and did well for a long time. I still remember that black velvet dress every time I see her in a movie.

I had hardly gotten my USC diploma when I went into the army. Frankly, when I got back from Cebu, I was all too ready to settle down for the steady life of the law student.

Hardly had I started studying civil procedure and torts when I was fixed up on a blind date with a lovely young woman from Mercedes, Texas, who had just that day landed a job at the *Pasadena Star-News*. We went to a dinner dance at the Riviera Country Club in Pacific Palisades, talked until late at night, and were married eight weeks later. She never started her job at the newspaper.

It would be impossible for me to adequately describe how important, how crucial, Mickey has been in my life. In fact, it is almost impossible for me to think of any kind of life except "our life." Her belief in me, her offering her strength and determination to me, made it possible for me to do every good thing that has ever happened to me. I still remember perfectly when I was a third-year law student about to take exams and came down with a severe flu. Mickey sat next to me in bed and read the course summaries to me in her soft, perfectly enunciated southern accent. It was her determination that I could make a law career by myself that made me strike out on my own to start my own small firm and become poised for the bench. Simply put, I cannot imagine how or what my life would have been without Mickey to sometimes support me, sometimes lead me, always be my partner.

I make quick decisions sometimes, and that one was not only quick, but the best one I ever made. *Brown* v. *Board of Education, Marbury* v. *Madison, Terry* v. *Ohio, Miranda, Escobedo*, all of them were and are important decisions in the life of this lawyer and this judge. But asking Mickey to marry me was by all odds the key to my having a quality life.

For a few years after law school, I practiced in a general commercial practice with my father—contracts, torts, negotiations. Then I went out on my own for several more years. In 1959, I was appointed a Municipal Court judge, and in 1961, I became a Superior Court judge.

As I said, a judge is first and foremost a human being. When my grandson, Ariel, came into the world, I thought about how the life of a human being is shaped by factors over which he has no control, or very little. If my father had not been a lawyer and taught me about the beauty of the law standing up for the little guy, if he had not taught me by example the drill of argumentation and persuasion, if Lana Turner had not flirted with other boys at the dance and (I am sure) ruined my rehearsal as Mr. Tallant, I might very well have become an actor—or at least tried.

If my mother had not sent me those tin cans of tuna which stopped a Japanese sniper's bullet back on Cebu, I might well be in a military cemetery. If I had not met Mickey, I would surely not have had a comfortable, happy life and two wonderful sons and a lovely daughter.

Now, you might well say, "What does any of this have to do with the law? Every grandfather probably feels exactly the same way that you feel."

Exactly the point: To be able to understand enough about life to judge people, a judge has to have lived life. He has to know what the hard parts of a life are and what temptation is and what frustration is and what random chance is. He has to know where good intentions lead, and what motive and circumstance means in a man's life, or a woman's.

I like to think that I got to be a better judge as I traveled farther along life's path and knew more about life. I got to know how fragile and uncertain a thing life is, and how carefully it must be approached.

So I looked at my grandson, Ariel, and I thought that what I would wish for him is what I would wish for a judge: to live long enough, and see enough, and feel enough, to appreciate what an incredibly complex thing life is, and how law must touch it with the utmost thought and conscience. I hope that Ariel, like me, and like all grandfathers, has a life which allows him to reach out to other people's feelings—not through experience in a war, I pray—and touch them with compassion and strength.

The law is about life, and a grandparent's thoughts on a new grandson are about life. That's the connection.

That's the look behind the scenes at a judge's life as he writes a book.

CHAPTER
ELEVEN

Try the Impossible

Speaking of life experiences, and particularly a certain kind of life experience which begins with, "Can you believe the nerve of this guy?" there is the story of Luis Eccheverria and his friend Jose Ramos.

In May of 1968, the two neatly dressed men came to the manager of an apartment in shady, quiet Sherman Oaks. The men were there responding to an advertisement for the rental of a modest two-bedroom apartment, furnished with battered but still serviceable Naugahyde couches and Formica tables. The men told the resident manager that they were priests living in the community to do service with the poor. They needed a quiet, peaceful apartment where there would be no one to disturb their meditation and prayer. This solitary study and supplication often went on until late at night and began early in the day.

The potential renters wanted to make certain above all that there were no policemen in the building. "They have such irregular hours, and can be called to duty so suddenly," Mr. Eccheverria explained, "that they might disturb us while we are at prayer."

The manager was a religious woman herself. She watched

at least five different television ministries, and had literally dozens of illustrated Bibles around her own apartment. She assured Messrs. Eccheverria and Ramos that they would be undisturbed in their new apartment. "It's right next to mine," she told them, "and I myself spend a great deal of time at prayer."

The manager noticed that the "priests" themselves did a great deal of their coming and going late at night. She once asked the two men if their work involved feeding the needy. "Yes," Mr. Ramos said, "and lifting the scales from their eyes."

As she later told it, the manager also noticed powerful chemical smells coming from the apartment of the two holy men, and she once asked them if they were making unusual food. "We have to boil our vestments," she was told. "They are sacred, and no ordinary dry cleaner can touch them without bringing shame on our order. We regret the inconvenience," they added politely, "but sacred rules are sacred."

On the morning of July 10, 1968, the manager was making a breakfast of oatmeal in her kitchen when she was suddenly knocked to the floor by a powerful explosion. Her dishes were knocked down as well, and most of her windows were shattered. Almost immediately thereafter, sheets of flame came from the "priests'" apartment and the whole building was filled with dense smoke.

Los Angeles happens to have a world-class fire department, which sent men and trucks, and "knocked down" the flames within an hour. Messrs. Ramos and Eccheverria had left in a hurry. Then, in standard fire department procedure, the firemen inspected the apartment to see if there was any residual fire or any flammable materials that might suddenly go up in flames. The firemen also have the gruesome duty of looking for victims in such cases.

One fireman was walking through the still smoldering bedroom, so smoky that he had to wear a mask, when he came upon a partially ajar closet. He opened the closet and shined his flashlight inside. There, as the report later said, "he noticed quantities of what appeared to be machine guns, dynamite, and ammunition. With the dynamite was also a coil of fuse."

The fireman exited the apartment in a hurry and called the bomb squad. The bomb squad inspected the apartment and found more dynamite in the living room, three automatic .38 pistols with silencers in a kitchen cupboard, and over one thousand machine-gun shells in a barrel under a smoldering mattress.

"I guess these men aren't priests after all," the manager later told police.

In fact, when the men were found, they were identified from fingerprints and mug shots as habitual dealers in illegal arms, lately, in those stormy days of 1968, for political terrorists. The unmasked "priests" were convicted of the relatively small crimes of possession of machine guns and dynamite and silencers, plus reckless endangerment of the public health by keeping dynamite in an apartment.

The men appealed, and asked that their convictions be thrown out because the police had no legal reason to search their apartment.

You may well wonder how a lawyer could raise such a defense with a straight face. But in fact a lawyer did raise exactly such a defense, and argued enthusiastically that the Constitution of the United States required that Messrs.

Ramos and Eccheverria go free because of violations of the search and seizure clause of the Fourth Amendment.

At that time, in 1968, I was sitting pro tem as a justice of the Court of Appeals of California. My job, as an appellate court judge, was not to decide on any questions of fact or evidence. My sole job was to rule on whether, as a matter of the laws of the United States and California, policemen may search an apartment which has been gutted by a fire started by a huge explosion to see if there was anything suspicious inside, and whether, if machine guns and dynamite are found in such an apartment, they can be lawfully seized as evidence without waiting for a search warrant.

That was the easiest case I have ever had to decide. I applaud defense counsel for thinking of his novel approach on appeal. I also applaud him for giving me a chance to play "Can you top this?" whenever discussions of human gall come up. I also hope that the manager asks future tenants for references.

In the same vein was the life and trials of one Dudley South. Mr. Dudley South had a long history of jobs as an auto-body painter, a fender-and-body man, and even a termite inspector. Then, at about the same time in 1966 that he reached the age of forty, he had an idea for a new career. He had read in a magazine about the boom in financial counseling. He saw no reason why he, a man of experience, should not go into that brave new field and make some real money.

The very first thing Mr. South did was take all the money he had in the world, about eighty dollars, to a bank. He had the bank open an account for him. On the checks he had the name of the new account: "DUDLEY SOUTH ASSOCIATES,

FINANCIAL CONSULTANTS.'' The next thing he did was go to a local Oldsmobile dealer and buy a new Oldsmobile with a check. The salesman was so certain that anyone who was a "financial consultant" would have enough money in his account to cover the check that he allowed Mr. South to simply drive away in his new Delta 88.

Then, Mr. South went to the stereo department of the May Co. on Fairfax Avenue and Wilshire Boulevard. He bought the top-of-the-line Fisher stereo ensemble and, again, paid by check to a part-time sales clerk who was certain that anyone who was a real "financial consultant" would surely have enough money in the bank to pay for one measly stereo.

For good measure, Mr. South also visited the resident manager of his apartment building in West Los Angeles and paid for the next two months rent in advance. He explained that his new business was thriving, and that he certainly wanted to share the wealth with such fine people as his landlords.

One week later, at the extremely insistent request of the Oldsmobile dealer, Mr. South was arrested for the crime of issuing checks knowing that there were insufficient funds in his account to cover them.

Many people, especially many college students, do not know that knowingly issuing checks without sufficient funds to cover them is a crime. It is. The reason that there are so few prosecutions for it is that it takes a very special person like Mr. South to make a record so clear that the district attorney can show that defendant knew there were insufficient funds in his account to cover the drafts.

Mr. South was a card at trial as well. First, he fired his public defender. Then he rehired her. Then he failed to show up for hearings twelve times. On the thirteenth occasion, he showed, between the arms of two sheriffs, but asked for a continuance, which is the same as a postponement. He presented to the court a greasy sheet of unmarked paper, with a handwritten note that Dudley South ". . . suffers from very bad headaches and cannot attend court. . . ." The judge was Joseph A. Wapner. I had him put in County Jail until trial.

Under questioning by his attorney, Mr. South insisted that he was not guilty because he had actually put money orders for over twenty thousand dollars in his account, but that the bank must have "lost" them. He had gotten the twenty thousand dollars from one single very wealthy client who had greatly appreciated his advice about her investments, he further explained under cross-examination by the district attorney. He "could not recall" the woman's name. He did not know where she lived or worked. He could not recall where he had "bought the money order" or at what branch of the bank he had "bought" it.

He did recall that he had studied accounting in night school and was bound to be a very successful financial consultant if we would only overlook this small oversight. He also "could not recall" what had happened to his Oldsmobile.

Just as the trial was coming to an end, he stood up in court and told me that he was firing his attorney because she was not energetic enough in defending him.

I told him it was a little late for that and to sit down.

Mr. South, the public defender, and the prosecutor had waived a jury trial and trusted me to render a fair decision. I hope I did. "The only part of your story I find convincing is that you studied accounting," I said, "because we have your school records. That shows you know enough addition and subtraction to realize that if you have eighty dollars in an account and then write checks for eight thousand, you did something wrong. If a public defender has represented you for eight months and then you try to fire her in the last five minutes of the case, that's not going to count as deprivation of counsel. Nor is it going to happen. Guilty as charged, and try to remember what you did with the car before I impose sentence."

To his credit, Mr. South suddenly recalled that he had lent the car to a friend and could get it back right away if he could avoid jail.

Again, I had to admire his audacity. A judge gets to see men and women in all kinds of strange positions, and gets to hear some of the best excuses the human mind can create. When I checked a few years later, Mr. South was studying creative writing at San Quentin Writing School, planning a stab at success in Hollywood when he got out. The more I thought about it, the more I thought he might just have hit on the right career move at last. He already knew a great deal about acting. I feel certain that if I had been able to study dramatics under Mr. South back at Hollywood High, Mr. Kachel would surely have kept me in the senior class play. Maybe if I had taken a few lessons from Mr. South about self-assurance, I might even have been able to impress Lana Turner enough for her to go out with me again.

Lessons from the cases of Messrs. Ramos, Eccheverria, and South: In plain English, what I saw was that even after people do the most outrageously wrong acts, they have the capacity to assume postures of wounded self-righteousness. Or, to put it even more bluntly, human beings who have committed crimes can easily persuade themselves that *they* and not society are the victims. Or, to make it completely basic, people will sometimes tell any lie when it's a matter of saving themselves from just punishment.

As a spectator and as a former actor, I can marvel at human versatility. As a judge, I have to see through it and realize who has been hurt and who has done the hurting, and to make payment accordingly. It all involves truth, consequences, and many discouraging views of human nature. I hope Ariel sees better people.

CHAPTER TWELVE

A Teacher from Outer Space

*C*hris DeRenzy had a feeling about Miss Carter. True, he was only ten years old and a fifth grader at Gardner Elementary School in Hollywood, and Miss Carter was *ancient,* probably thirty at least, and she was the teacher, but still, Chris had a feeling.

First, there were the times that Miss Carter had showed up with her clothes dirty and torn, and told them that she was late because secret agents from the FBI were chasing her. Then, on other days, when she was late for the beginning of school and even so late that substitutes had to be called, Miss Carter explained to the students that she was doing secret assignments for the shah of Iran (this was in 1977).

Certainly, Chris had been brought up by his mother and father to respect grown-ups. And certainly he knew that he was no expert in secret agents. But he had read a number of comic books about secret agents, had watched three James Bond movies, had seen hundreds of hours of cartoons about spies. None of the spies he had seen on TV or in theaters or in comic books looked even slightly like Miss Carter. They all looked like they could do something. Miss Carter always looked as if she might come apart into small pieces. She also looked a fair amount like the wicked witch in his grandmother's favorite movie, *The Wizard of Oz*. She did not look like a spy at all.

What was worse, when she told them she was a spy, she didn't tell it as if it were a fairy tale or a joke. Chris loved tall tales, but at ten, he could almost always tell when a grown-up really believed the fairy tale herself, and Miss Carter definitely believed her own fairy tales.

Then there were the times that Miss Carter would suddenly cry out when she was teaching an arithmetic lesson and clutch her head. "It's happening again," she would say. "The police are beaming radar waves inside my brain to make me tell them what I know about the CIA." When she told the class about her headaches, she did not seem to be joking at all.

But the cruncher was when Miss Carter told Chris and his best friend Ruth that they would have to stay after school because they were interfering with her ability to concentrate on her plans for running for president. "How did we do that?" Chris had asked.

"Your brain waves are messing up my communication with my advisers in Washington," she told him. Chris had to stay for an hour when he would much rather have played football with his friends, and Ruth had to miss her favorite game show, "Jeopardy."

That was when Chris told his mother and father about his problems with Miss Carter. Many parents might not have taken a ten-year-old seriously when he told them his teacher was insane (because that was the feeling that Chris had) but his parents were unusual. For one thing, his father was a psychiatrist. For another thing, his mother was a psychiatrist as well. But the main thing was that they trusted their son. He was not a liar and he did not make up stories that might hurt people or get them in trouble.

Chris's parents went to see Mrs. Zeller, the principal of Gardner Elementary School. Mrs. Zeller might normally have pooh-poohed questions about a teacher's sanity. But since, one day before, she had gotten a letter from Miss Carter which read in part, "I know you are bombarding my house with microwaves to try to make me forget all that the shah told me . . ." Mrs. Zeller was concerned herself.

She started to ask the other faculty members about Miss Carter. She also made careful notes about what Chris had told her. The returns from the faculty were interesting. One member told about how Miss Carter had told him that she did not like to breathe in Los Angeles, because germs carried on air currents from China might infect her, and her body would be unable to fight off germs from China. Another teacher told her about Miss Carter claiming to have been married to the then President, Jimmy Carter. "In fact, I'm still married to him," she had said, "and I'm having his baby. It's a secret. I have a lot of secrets."

Mrs. Zeller thought about Miss Carter for some weeks, and then she decided that perhaps the board of education should be made aware of some of Miss Carter's secrets. When the board heard about Miss Carter, they were very impressed with her connections with President Carter and the shah. They placed her on immediate involuntary sick leave and recommended that she get psychiatric help as soon as she could take time off from her work for the shah.

Miss Carter did not take this lying down. She hired a lawyer and sued the school board for reinstatement, claiming that there was inadequate evidence that she had in fact shown symptoms of mental illness. The board said that she could be examined by three independent psychiatrists who would then render an opinion. The psychiatrists were shown Miss Carter's personnel files so that they would know what specific symptoms to look for.

The psychiatrists spoke to Miss Carter for two hours, discussed her case among themselves, and came back with a verdict: Chris DeRenzy was right. Miss Carter was suffering from severe paranoid delusions and abnormal affect. To entrust to her personality the teaching of young children was the height of irresponsibility.

The school board confirmed Miss Carter's involuntary sick leave. However, Miss Carter (no doubt energized by certain radio waves) went into my court and demanded that she be returned to her duties (by which she meant her duties for the school board and not her duties for the CIA, I assume).

I heard the case, watched Miss Carter on the stand, heard the teachers, even heard Chris, and then examined the psychiatrists. Miss Carter's lawyers had waived a jury, so I was required to decide all issues of fact and law.

During the recesses, when I thought about the case, I carefully considered all of the facts and what I had seen and heard. I also read California's laws on ordering teachers to take involuntary sick leave. But I also thought about something else. The ordinary citizen may well think that law is boring, and sometimes it is, to be frank. But what I, as a judge, got to see day after day was the most fascinating parade of humanity imaginable. My older son, Fred, had just graduated from McGeorge Law School in Sacramento. My younger son Dave had just entered Loyola Law School.

I was happy for them, happy for me that I got to see not just one small slice of the human comedy and tragedy, but the whole spectrum of human sorrow and triumph. The law touches absolutely everything, and lawyers get to see it all if they stay in the field long enough.

(Well, maybe the law does not touch absolutely everything: The law does not have much connection with people who are perfectly happy and never get into arguments with anyone. But then how many people like that are there?)

To be fair to Miss Carter, she raised an excellent point: Should her personnel files be opened to the psychiatrists, or would the information in them prejudice the doctors so that they could not fairly resolve her case? Moreover, was the information in those files not hearsay, and therefore inadmissible in court?

These were major concerns. We all want teachers to feel as if their records are confidential. We also want to keep hearsay, the unexamined statements of persons, out of court, out of the trial process, although, of course, there are many exceptions to the hearsay rule such as those involving expert witnesses who may render opinions based on hearsay (and others too numerous to mention).

But, as always, there were other concerns. We want our teachers to be sane. And we want the psychiatrists to have some idea of what they are looking for when they examine a teacher. I decided that the school board had not erred in showing Miss Carter's personnel files to the three-psychiatrist panel and confirmed the decision by the school board.

Miss Carter, a tireless woman to be sure, appealed my decision, but it was upheld by the California Court of Appeals.

My heart went out to Miss Carter. It is not pleasant to be shackled by paranoid delusions as far as I have been able to observe. Sometimes, however, even sad facts of human life are so outlandish that a judge has to laugh despite himself. As it happened, Miss Carter responded extremely well to therapy and was successfully back at work within three years, so it all turned out well.

As for Chris, he should be proud. Probably every student thinks at some time that his teachers are crazy. Chris DeRenzy had the satisfaction of having his feelings upheld by the school board and by a superior court and by the court of appeals. I hope it did not go to his head.

I owe something to Chris as well. He recalled to me the truth that those who look beneath a word like "teacher" or "student" to the more important word "truth" are the ones to whom the law needs to listen.

CHAPTER THIRTEEN

A Naked Right

Speaking of human comedy, there is the case of Eden Incorporated and *Nude Look*.

Los Angeles is an extremely unusual county. It includes downtown Los Angeles, where there are blocks of fifty- and sixty-story buildings. It also includes hundreds of square miles of sprawling suburbs. Unknown to many persons outside L.A., it also includes rugged, completely rural canyons and ravines. Sometimes those canyons and arroyos go on for dozens of miles. When my children were young, I often went with Mickey and the kids to picnic in one or another of them, either Malibu Canyon or Topanga Canyon—which later became famous because Charles Manson had lived there for a time with his infamous "family."

Also in Topanga Canyon was a far more wholesome enterprise. A group of nudists had bought thirty acres, landscaped it, put in tennis courts, buildings, and a Jacuzzi, and created "The Garden of Eden," as I will call it, a place where men and women could take off their clothes and feel happy in the California sunshine.

For a small fee, anyone could join The Garden of Eden.

Soon, the organization had thousands of members who might attend religiously, so to speak, or might only go once in a lifetime to see what life was like in paradise.

The organization was so successful and had so many members that the leadership of The Garden of Eden decided that it might be smart to have a newsletter or even a modest magazine. That magazine might have photos of some of the more comely inhabitants of The Garden of Eden in some of their more alluring poses, along with descriptions of the activities of the nice people of The Garden of Eden.

In about 1964, the governors of the group decided to call their magazine *Nude Look*. They printed several issues and distributed them to their members.

There was a problem with *Nude Look*, however. At that time (in 1964), there was a very large magazine published by Cowles Magazines entitled *Look*. The people who ran Cowles were not at all happy with a magazine called *Nude Look*. They thought it might confuse people about which magazine was which. They also thought it mocked their magazine and also that it stole *Look* magazine's good name and goodwill.

In early 1964, the lawyers for Cowles went into Superior Court. They asked for and got an injunction restraining Garden of Eden from publishing *Nude Look*. The grounds were that further publication would do irreparable harm to the good name of *Look*. Injunctions are a form of what is called "equitable" relief. That relief almost always requires the doing or not doing of a specific thing as compared with the payment of money damages. Usually, in fact, almost always, equitable relief is ordered by a court only if the court believes that money damages would not be adequate to make a defendant whole. For example, if I owned a priceless, perfect Victorian house and the state wanted to exercise its right of eminent domain and knock it down to build a freeway, I might apply for an injunction barring the city from knocking it down. The theory would be that no amount of money could replace a perfect old Victorian, and so the court might need to order an immediate remedy like moving the house to a new location. Injunctive relief often, but not always, involves real estate.

Garden of Eden leaders, who knew what it was like to defy established authority, continued to publish *Nude Look*. Cowles went into the same Superior Court and demanded that Garden of Eden pay a fine. The court so ordered.

Garden of Eden paid the fine (a small amount in any event) and then appealed the injunction and the imposition of the fine. They said that their First Amendment rights were being abridged, and that the damage to the good name of *Look* was so conjectural and hypothetical as to scarcely require depriving Garden of Eden of its rights under the Constitution. The judge took a look at *Look* and then took a look at *Nude Look* and gave the verdict to the Garden of Eden.

Amazingly, however, the court refused to refund the fine, even after acknowledging that the injunction should never have been issued and dissolving the injunction. The Garden of Eden appealed to the California Court of Appeals, on which I was then sitting pro tem.

Frankly, the legal issues involved were extremely clear cut. When a court had ordered a fine paid pursuant to a judicial order later found to be invalid, the fine must be returned. That much was clear enough. I ordered the fine repaid, with interest. I am sure the lower court was sincere, but simply made an honest mistake.

But the basic outline of what had happened was clear enough. It shows something about how the world works. Even a giant corporation, known and looked up to throughout the world for the quality of its work, can be extremely petty when it thinks that money is involved. Even a huge, highly visible communications company can try to block others out of the light of the First Amendment. The fact of size and prestige does not in any sense equate with being right or following the Constitution.

I also learned something else: "A fine is not fine when a *Look* is not a *Nude Look*." File that away among Wapner's principles of law.

CHAPTER FOURTEEN

Runaround

*E*xercise is a gift to mankind. It enhances our health, helps our hearts pump more blood more easily, fills our red cells with oxygen, makes us slim and lean, and, just as important, makes us feel better. That is, we not only feel better about taking care of our bodies, but we actually feel better, more at peace, even exhilarated. The exercise craze hit this country in the early seventies, by my recollection, but many people had exercised regularly for some time before that.

I have played tennis regularly for thirty years. If I miss a scheduled game of tennis, I feel irritable and upset. My wife and my whole family have known for some time that they are happier when I am happy, and that means—in part— regular exercise.

Of all the exercise regimens which have taken hold in America, none has grown so fast or taken such a tenacious grip on America as running. Twenty years ago, only a few people ran, and they were thought of as decidedly off the beaten track unless they were still in school.

But today, tens of millions of Americans run regularly. Middle-aged people, elderly people, even pregnant women exercise by running or at least jogging through rain and heat and snow. Running shoes have become a multibillion-dollar business and sports medicine has become a huge specialty.

Here in Los Angeles, running is particularly popular. Because the weather is pleasant year round, because people here, both men and women, are fixated on their appearance, running has become a virtual obsession. On any day on any broad street, you can see men and women trotting down the median strip, hoping against hope to run their way to beauty, or at least to feeling good about their lives.

Marathon running has become popular here, and there are all kinds of other ways of running in competition as well.

The Los Angeles Athletic Club, one of the oldest and finest athletic clubs in America, has for the past decade sponsored a particularly interesting form of running competition. The LAAC sets aside one month each year for the contest. The terms of the event are that any member, male or female, may run as many miles per day for that month as he or she can manage. The runners may rack up their mileage at the club's indoor track at Sixth and Olive downtown, or they may run anywhere they wish and record their miles each day on the honor system. Runners tend to be an exacting and self-disciplined lot, so LAAC had never had any trouble with the honor system until 1980 or thereabouts.

In that year, a woman whom I will call Leslie Wilson was determined to win. She was in her early thirties and had been running seriously since she was a teenager. She lived near a large park in Whittier, a suburb southeast of downtown, and she ran there every day. She was in excellent physical condition, and she was able to run as much as ten or twelve miles day after day. As any runner can tell you, that is a major accomplishment.

Leslie Wilson's husband was also a dedicated runner. He was himself a competitor in the men's race, and took it at least as seriously as Leslie. Sam Wilson was in the oil business, and in that year of 1980, he was making money hand over fist. To win the running competition, or at least see his wife win it, would round out a perfect year.

For the first fifteen days of the competition, everything was going according to Leslie Wilson's hopes. She was sweating blood, but she was chalking up twelve miles each and every day. No one else was even close to her mark. All of her sacrifice and pain at the Whittier College stadium had indeed paid off, or so it seemed.

Then, quite abruptly, in the next few days everything changed. A woman runner whom Leslie had never heard of, whom I will call Svetlana Jones, started to record daily runs of twenty-eight to thirty miles per day. Day after day for a week, she was writing down that she had run truly heroic distances.

Sam Wilson was concerned. He asked about Svetlana Jones at the club. No one knew anything about her except that she was a member. There was no memory of her being a particularly great runner. In fact, hardly anyone could even tell Sam Wilson what Svetlana Jones looked like.

Six days before the end of the month, Svetlana Jones had recorded a total mileage of almost nine hundred miles and Leslie Wilson was not even close to winning any longer.

Sam Wilson was skeptical, to put it mildly. A total mileage of nine hundred was simply unheard of for amateurs. For all of it to have been recorded on the honor system compounded his suspicions. He sprang into action.

He called his lawyer. "I don't care what it costs," he said. "Hire a private investigator and find out who this Svetlana Jones is and if she possibly is running that kind of mileage."

The lawyer reluctantly hired a PI, who watched Svetlana, staked her out, so to speak, for a few days at the end of the competition. The private investigator not only followed her himself, but also had replacements watch her when he went off duty, to make sure she was not by any chance running her miles in the middle of the night.

The private investigator reported to the lawyer and the lawyer reported to Mr. Wilson. The basic report was simple: Ms. Jones was raising a family, working at a job, and maybe running a few hundred yards in the morning to catch a bus. She did not appear to be the slightest bit fatigued at any time the PI watched her.

The bottom line: As far as the PI could tell, those miles Svetlana Jones chalked up were simply made up.

Sam Wilson told his lawyer to do whatever he possibly could do to keep the club from awarding the medal to Ms. Jones. "My wife won that thing," he said. "I won't see her cheated out of it."

The lawyer was not at all enthusiastic about the case. It was a dicey business to ask a court to take jurisdiction of a running contest at a private club. Courts usually do not get involved in such things. Courts do not like to enter relationships between private citizens unless there is a clear legal cause of action or a law which has been violated.

But the lawyer was resourceful even if unenthusiastic. He scoured the California and Los Angeles codes, and especially the business and professional codes. He found a few obscure provisions about contests and promotions and how they had to be on the up and up. It was a long shot, but he hurriedly went into Superior Court and asked for a ruling that the running competition was so clearly not reaching a fair result, had so evidently not been won by the prescribed means, that to give Ms. Jones the award would be a violation of the law.

Amazing as it may seem, the court agreed and gave a preliminary injunction to Sam Wilson. The club was prevented by court order from giving the running trophy to Svetlana Jones.

As you might imagine, Svetlana Jones was not happy. No one likes to be called a liar and a cheat as far as I have ever been able to tell. To be called a fraud in one's own club and then to have it in the newspapers as well is pure humiliation.

Svetlana sued to get "her" trophy. The LAAC stepped out of the whole mess and just told the court that it would abide by the court's decision. There were motions and memos and briefs for two and a half years before the Superior Court. Even for Sam Wilson, the case was getting expensive. For Svetlana, it was becoming overwhelming.

That was when yours truly got involved in the case. By 1982, I was retired from the bench, happily playing tennis almost every day, and just beginning my career resolving disputes on television.

However, when you have been resolving differences between persons for more than twenty years, you get into the habit of being a judge. Like many retired judges, I was available for special judicial assignments in resolving legal matters without the formality of a court trial.

By this I mean that if the parties to a case agreed, the case could be taken out of the formal confines of Superior Court and assigned to me as a judge "by order of reference" or as a judge "pro tem" under the California Constitution. The parties would put on their case before me in a more informal manner than if they were at the Superior Court Building. I would hear testimony and witnesses would be examined and cross-examined by counsel and then I would reach a decision and render an order. (This is an extremely effective mode of settling cases and getting them disposed of quickly, and I applaud it.)

First, the Wilson team put on witnesses who were experienced, nationally recognized runners—although, frankly, I had not heard of them. The runners testified as to what happened to their bodies if they ran ten or twelve miles per day, not to mention twenty-eight to thirty miles per day. Their bodies became taut and lean, even emaciated. Photos of Svetlana at the time of the competition showed someone who looked a lot more like Miss Piggy than like a dense ball of muscle and faith.

Then the Wilson lawyer put on doctors who testified about what a toll running twenty-eight to thirty miles per day would take out of a person. The doctors made the same point—that for Miss Svetlana Jones to have run the mileage she claimed would have been very close to physiologically impossible. Certainly, it would not have been possible while the woman also worked and raised a family.

Finally, the lawyer for Leslie and Sam Wilson produced evidence that Svetlana Jones had a history of being discharged from her jobs under questionable circumstances involving false expense accounting. None of the Wilson evidence purported to show that she was a felon, and I certainly did not take it that way, but clearly, it looked extremely grim for Ms. Svetlana Jones.

Her case primarily took the form of "either you trust me

or you don't, and if you don't then you've hurt my feelings. . . ." While this may be a persuasive tack for a third grader to take with her mother, it did not work with me.

The bottom line, as far as I could tell, was that Svetlana Jones had indeed falsified her mileage. To my mind, she was similar to the woman who had won the Boston Marathon in 1980, Rosie Ruiz, and had set a record time. It turned out that she had been ducking into the subway and taking an express train for long portions of the ride, then emerging, blending in with the crowd, and winning by miles.

I turned to Svetlana Jones. "Young lady," I told her, "I hate to say this. But you are a fraud."

I ordered that the trophy for the month-long competition be awarded to Leslie Wilson. The Los Angeles Athletic Club was sportsmanlike about it, as I knew it would be.

The club convened a special awards ceremony just for Leslie Wilson. She had a medal hung around her neck while the club's runners applauded. To my mind, she indeed deserved the medal. She and her husband had run more than a marathon on their feet, on tracks indoors and outdoors. They also had the imagination and tenacity to run a legal race and stay with it until the trophy was theirs. That's grit, and that especially is a husband who believes in his wife.

As for Ms. Svetlana Jones, perhaps she will remember that it's good to run, and it's sometimes good to run around. But it's not good to try to give the Los Angeles Athletic Club—or a judge—a runaround.

Even when money is not involved, even when great events like strikes or building highways are not involved, a judge can still perform a huge service by bringing his eyes and ears and basic common sense into a situation. The law is not just for prescribed causes of action like divorces or robberies or wills and estates. The law is for any conflict where human beings need another sensitive human being to hear the facts and mete out fairness. The law is as much about cheating in long-distance running as in price-fixing or robbing a bank. Law is fairness in action, for Leslie Wilson or General Motors or anyone under the Constitution.

CHAPTER FIFTEEN

One Fortunate Cookie

Wang Ho was trying his best to be a good American. His parents had escaped from China to the United States in 1949, bringing him with them. He had gone to Los Angeles High School and then gotten a job as an accountant in the Los Angeles Rapid Transit District, which supervises our city's extremely wayward buses. Still, Mr. Ho had nothing to do with the observed fact that our L.A. buses crash into cars at about ten times the national average. Instead, he methodically tallied up columns of data about ridership and the relationship of ridership to time of day and route, and then entered this data on a roll of computer tape. What use was made of it was beyond his control and even his interest.

What did interest Wang Ho, as well as his wife, Anne Ho, was American movies. They loved all kinds of American films, from horror movies to romance to science fiction. But most of all, they loved gangster movies. To Wang Ho, toiling at his desk at the Rapid Transit District's dull gray headquarters downtown, the life of gangsters was the perfect life of an American. They were able to shoot people whenever they felt like it. They always had beautiful girls on their arms. They even had more money than they knew what to do with. With that money, the gangsters could buy Cadillacs, pay tips to headwaiters, and wear solid gold cuff links. How could you beat that?

By early 1973, Mr. Ho and Anne Ho had seen *The Godfather* three times. But they still thought it was no better than a Depression-era gangster movie called *Public Enemy*, with the immortal Jimmy Cagney. One night in May 1973, to their delight, the Hos found that *Public Enemy* was playing on television. They had to see it. To make sure they were uninterrupted, they decided to leave their eighteen-month-old son, Jason Ho, upstairs in his playpen with his favorite toy, a large unopened bottle of 7-Up.

Alas, some time after Cagney made the big time in the movie, the Hos heard crying from Jason's room. They ran in to see that Jason had suffered an accident with his 7-Up. He had bitten off a part of the metal cap, then scratched his eye with it. The scratch was a bad one, and when Wang and Anne Ho came into his room, Jason's eye looked like something out of *Alien*.

The Hos rushed Jason to the hospital, where they were told that his eye was not permanently hurt, but that he would require a long and expensive period of convalescence.

The Hos decided that it was not their fault, but the fault of the Seven-Up Company for making caps so dangerous that an eighteen-month-old left alone with a large bottle of 7-Up might hurt himself. The Hos sued.

Even in a child-centered nation like ours, eighteen-month-olds are not allowed to sue by themselves in court. (For one thing, how could they see over the counsel table to raise objections?) A guardian "ad litem" (for litigation, loosely) must be appointed. Normally, that would be the father or mother, and I allowed Wang Ho to be guardian ad litem for Jason Ho's suit against the Seven-Up Company.

As with all civil trials—and I will have much more to say about this later—I tried to encourage a settlement before the case went to trial. Mr. Ho had a capable, thoughtful attorney who also wanted a settlement. The lawyer for 7-Up offered a settlement of $5,000 right off the bat. To me, that did not seem a bad settlement in itself. It was not clear that the negligence, if there were any, was 7-Up's rather than the senior Hos for leaving their infant son unattended with a large bottle of 7-Up.

However, Mr. Ho had apparently learned stubbornness from Jimmy Cagney and Al Pacino. He sneered at the offer and simply refused even to think about it. After further discussion, the lawyer for 7-Up offered $22,500 as a final attempt at pretrial settlement. It seemed like a generous offer indeed.

"Mr. Ho," I said in chambers, "you can never predict what will happen in a jury case. You would be wise to accept this settlement offer."

In his best imitation of the fading Don Corleone, Wang Ho told me that it was ". . . out of the question. . . ." At this point, he told me with a straight face, ". . . it has become a question of the honor of my family."

I thought about the honor of Mr. Ho's family, about his leaving his one-and-a-half-year-old son in his room alone with a large bottle of 7-Up, and then I spoke frankly to Mr. Ho and his lawyer and the defendant's lawyer.

"Mr. Ho," I said, "I'm going to make you an offer you can't refuse. If you don't come to your senses about this case, I'm going to remove you as guardian ad litem for young Jason and put in someone who'll listen to reason."

Showing complete composure Al Pacino–style, Mr. Ho said he would think about it and consult with his family— as if "his family" were the ganglords of all of the East Coast instead of his wife Anne Ho. I despaired of getting anywhere with him and started to mentally prepare an order removing him as guardian ad litem.

But to my surprise and delight, Mr. Ho appeared in chambers the next morning with his lawyer. I summoned the Seven-Up lawyer and we had a conference.

Still using his hoarse movie idol voice, Wang Ho told me that he had decided to accept the settlement. "Why?" I asked. "What made you change your mind?"

"Because my wife and I took Jason out to a Chinese restaurant for dinner last night. After dinner, Jason got a fortune cookie that I opened for him. It said, 'Lean settlement better than fat lawsuit.' I feel as if Somebody is telling me something."

"Someone is," I told him. "Someone is telling you that you just did the smartest thing you could have done. Good luck and good-bye."

He made his hand into a pistol, put down his thumb hammer, winked, and left my chambers.

The very first thing I did when Mr. Ho and the lawyers had gone was to tell the story to my clerk, Betty Jung. "Call all the Chinese food wholesalers in town," I said. "Find out how I can get a whole bag of those fortune cookies with the same message about 'lean settlements' and 'fat lawsuits' and get them to my chambers. Quick."

I use those fortune cookies all the time. If potential litigants knew how much better off they almost always are by settling than by going into a long, expensive, totally unpredictable lawsuit, there would be a great many more settlements, much shorter lines at the windows of justice, and a lot less expense for taxpayers. Fortune cookies obviously are not the answer to the litigation explosion. But settlement is such a good idea, and protracted litigation is almost always such a bad idea, that I'll try those cookies to help people see the light.

Plus, they taste good.

CHAPTER
SIXTEEN

Settlements and Common Sense

When most Americans imagine a lawsuit, they may imagine several different scenarios. They might think of Perry Mason striding back and forth before the jury box, suddenly noticing Paul Drake rush into court, and then confronting a widow with evidence of her complicity in murder. Or, they might imagine the litigants in "People's Court," appearing for their brief time in court, explaining their position succinctly to a judge who then rapidly makes up his mind and dispenses (what I hope is) a fair result. The ordinary citizen might even think of the appearance at a long oak bench of the nine justices of the United States Supreme Court, deciding issues of great moment from integration to criminal procedure, with forty seconds of comment by a network commentator standing in the snow or the sun in front of the majestic columns of that Court.

All of those are valid pictures of the legal process. But in fact each shows only the most interesting, most dramatic part of that process.

In real life, for most civil cases, that is, cases where no criminal penalties are involved but only disputes involving money and property, the legal process is far more ordinary.

Generally speaking, a person who feels aggrieved begins a case by hiring a lawyer. The lawyer then informs himself of the facts of the case. Then he tries to learn what legal standards apply to the case. Then he applies the legal theory he has found to the facts of the case. He draws up a complaint which summarizes the facts of the case in such a way as to state a "cause of action."

By that I mean that the facts must fall into some legally recognizable form of lawsuit. For example, if one went to a lawyer and said, "I hate my job because it's so boring, and I want to sue my boss for being so boring," any lawyer would have to say that there are no grounds for a lawsuit. The law does not recognize being boring as a grounds for legal action.

However, if a woman goes to her lawyer and says, "I was asked to have sex by my boss, and when I refused, he fired me," the lawyer could draw up a complaint. The law recognizes sexual harassment as a cause of action.

Once the cause of action has been found and the complaint drawn up and filed, then the person who is being sued sees his lawyer. Usually, the client and the lawyer deny the facts of the allegation, or at least some of the facts. Often, the lawyer also denies that what the plaintiff (the one who sues) alleges constitutes a legal cause of action even if the facts are true.

For example, a screenwriter may allege that a studio stole her idea for a movie and then made it into a movie without paying her. The studio may respond by saying that it did not steal the writer's idea, that it had never even heard of the writer, *but* that even if it used a similar idea to the writer's idea, and even if it had heard of her, "mere" ideas are not able to be copyrighted or legally recognized and therefore the law has no interest in the matter.

Often, there is oral argument and a hearing just on the question of whether there is a legal cause of action in a lawsuit. Just preparing papers for such a hearing can take weeks or months.

This is just the beginning.

If the lawsuit proceeds beyond the issue of whether there is a legally recognizable issue, then there is "discovery." There are requests for documents such as medical records or memoranda within a corporation. There are mini-inquisitions in which witnesses and potential witnesses are "deposed" and asked if they plan to say certain things at the trial. Then there are still more arguments about who can be deposed, what documents must be produced, and who can schedule a deposition where.

This process can take weeks, months, and even years.

In the meanwhile, the lawyers' meters are running. Even the very least expensive lawyer charges about one hundred dollars per hour for his time. Legal fees vary depending on the part of the country involved and the legal specialty called upon, but such fees can easily range up to four hundred dollars per hour, and sometimes even higher than that for time spent in court. Even if a plaintiff's lawyer is getting paid on a contingent fee basis, he is accumulating expenses for paralegals, for photocopying, for secretarial work, for transportation. Also, while the plaintiff's lawyer may be on a contingent fee basis, the defendant's lawyer almost never is, and his time is expensive as well.

Before a case even gets close to a trial, the litigants can have spent huge sums, invested great amounts of their time, and become mentally and physically exhausted.

Then, when they get to a jury, the jury can behave completely unpredictably. For any whim that strikes any juror, a perfectly good case can be tossed out the window, or a terrible case may be found valid.

As for me, I am horrified by the expense, aggravation, and uncertainty in all too many trials. Yes, it is vital to have a legal system with adequate safeguards of constitutional rights. But no, it is not always the best, fastest, most efficient way to dispense justice to have a process that consumes vast amounts of money, time, and human energy and then comes down to a roll of the dice in far too many cases.

For those reasons, and for others, I have been and still am an eager advocate of settlements. The case of Wang Ho and his son Jason was only one small example. My experience has been that if human beings can face each other and communicate with each other in an atmosphere where they can confidently expect justice, they can avoid trial and save everyone money, time, and trouble.

A settlement is almost always preferable to a trial, and that is the most basic of legal truths.

But settlements are often inhibited by an equally basic problem: When human beings are in conflict, they cannot agree on the right settlement. That is why they are suing in the first place. If they could just sit down and agree, there would never be any complaints, hearings, depositions, or any of the other creaking machinery of the legal process. Human beings in conflict in the legal system are appealing to someone else to hear the facts and then render an impartial opinion. That is why they put their cases before judges and juries.

I have always believed, for as long as I have been a judge, that if litigants could put their problems simply and clearly before a person they trusted and ask that person for a judgment, they could save most of the rigmarole of the formal, drawn-out legal process.

For as long as I was a sitting judge, I tried to be that person. Even after I retired from the bench, I made myself available to resolve disputes in an informal, expedited way. I tried to make myself into a figure who could hear the most important facts of a case and then render a decision with which both sides could feel contented, if not actually happy.

To put all of this more simply, if plaintiff and defendant could feel that they just had a man or a woman whom they could talk to about their case, then trust that man or woman to behave with fairness in the outcome, they would not constantly have to hedge their bets with all manner of legal puts and calls, and I have tried my damnedest to be such a person.

It did not always work. There were cases where the litigants had to fight it out to the bitter end—sometimes to the bitter end of their solvency. But little by little, I started to get a certain kind of reputation as a man who could be trusted. That reputation made it possible for lawyers and their clients to trust me rather than play out the legal system unto the last syllable of recorded time. There were certainly other jurists who knew more about Delaware Civil Procedure than I did, in case anyone in California needed to know about Delaware Civil Procedure. There may well have been judges who knew better about the relationship of law and economics or other new studies in law. But I was a judge whom people could trust to see problems to their heart and offer a fair resolution. That was the reputation I cherished.

To be honest, I was emotionally and mentally predisposed to like settlements better than lawsuits. First of all, I am impatient. I know that's a flaw, but it is still there, a deeply embedded flaw. As an impatient man, I chafe at seeing endless witnesses, arguments about procedure, disputes over trivia. I like to get cases moving toward a fair conclusion. To me, that is what law is all about. Certainly, it is what I am all about.

Second, I am not a passive person. It is difficult for me to just sit back on the bench and play referee while the two sides duke it out. My natural predilection is to get into the ring myself and help to pound out a settlement. There is far more scope for me to work on a dispute as settler of the case than as judge. So, to be perfectly honest about it, I enjoy settling cases more than sitting quietly listening to week after week of testimony.

Now, one of the advantages of growing up in a home where my father was a lawyer and everyone was argumentative and outspoken was that you learn debater's techniques firsthand—and early. I got to see that a truly ingenious person can argue any side of an issue and find convincing material and even emotional commitment.

That helped me to understand that just because people argued a brief or an issue passionately, their passion did not make them right. Their marshaling of facts and logic did not even make them necessarily right. I knew that I could make an argument out of anything, and so could the persons before me.

By the same token, I learned at home to see both sides of an argument—or more than two sides if necessary. I could put myself into the shoes of either party to an argument and see where he had truly strong points and where he was clearly working with whole cloth. This, too, helped me to see to the heart of cases and understand where there was something real and where there was not.

But perhaps most of all, as the result of having seen where conflict between *nations* leads, I could see that there was not only a financial cost to disputes, but a human cost. I wanted to be able to put those human costs right up at the front of the docket and work to minimize them on both sides.

To make the point, think of the difference between surgeons and butchers.

In 1948, when I was taking the California Bar, I experienced cruel pain in my back. I went to the Veterans Administration Hospital in Westwood and had my back fluoroscoped. As you might have guessed, the fluoroscope revealed, and the X rays confirmed, that I had a piece of Made in Japan shrapnel still in my upper back. I went in for surgery to have it removed. The nurse gave me a shot of local anesthetic and then the doctor cut into my back with his scalpel.

After a few moments of cutting, he said, "I don't see a thing. It's not here."

I was lying on my stomach, very groggy, but I said, "Well, why don't you consult the X rays and see where it is?"

Very grudgingly, he looked at the X rays, harrumphed, and then cut in an entirely different place. Sure enough, there was the shrapnel. He removed it, put it on a tray, and the nurse handed it to me to view. Then the doctor started to sew me up. Incredibly, he paused and turned to his pretty nurse. "Here," he said, "you've never done this before. Perhaps you'd like to practice on Lieutenant Wapner."

If I had not been so doped up, I would have punched him in the nose. My back is not a practice field for the nursing team.

No sooner had I gotten home than the flimsy bandage which the doctor had applied fell off and onto the floor. I called the doctor to ask him what to do. "Just put it back on," he said.

"But it was on the floor," I answered. "My wife keeps a clean house, but it's not sterile."

The doctor sighed contemptuously. "All right," he said. "Come back in and I'll put on another bandage."

I went in. After much waiting, the doctor put me on my stomach and examined my wound. "Wow," he said, "a great big hematoma!" A hematoma is a large blood clot, which you are not supposed to get if your surgery had been done properly and if your wound has been sewn up and bandaged properly.

With barely disguised glee, moving much more enthusiastically than when I had first seen him, the doctor took out a scalpel and, with no anesthesia whatsoever, sliced right through the clot.

You can imagine the results. Blood spattered throughout the room, onto the walls, the ceiling, everywhere, even in my hair. The doctor laughed.

That experience taught me a great deal. First, it showed me that men who have a title or a degree may not have any more than that. (Chris DeRenzy could have probably told me that as well, but he was not yet born in 1948.) The fact that a man has an M.D. does not in any sense insure that he is a caring man or even necessarily a healing man.

But second, and far more important, that experience told me something about the human costs of procedures. I had to have that piece of shrapnel removed. In the end, it got removed. But the doctor who removed it did so callously and without regard to the fact that he was operating not on a rubber dummy but on a real-life human being with nerve endings, hopes, and fears.

I tried hard to think about that when I was on the bench. A lawsuit is a procedure not wildly dissimilar from a medical procedure. It can be done so as to minimize the pain attendant upon cutting and stitching, or it can be done so that the court does not give a goddamn about the pain of the people before him.

To my way of thinking, when a lawsuit goes into long depositions, arguments over petty procedural matters, and exponentially increasing bitterness and cost, that is the equivalent of sloppy, careless surgery unless it absolutely cannot be avoided. When a judge simply allows the lawyers to run away with a case and exhaust every legal procedure before getting justice, that shows disregard for the human costs of litigation.

(I might add that any reader who has ever been in protracted litigation knows precisely what I am talking about. Every reader who has never been in litigation should think of being in surgery and then imagine the surgery going on for months, and he will have an idea of what litigation is like. Every reader who has never had either surgery or litigation might imagine getting stuck in traffic while en route to a job interview, to get the picture. Litigation is a whole new experience in anxiety for the ordinary citizen.)

I tried very hard to make every possible effort to settle cases before the pain got too intense and before the hematoma of procedural wrangling set in.

In other words, to get past the bloodstained motivations, I was a highly driven man when it came to settlements. As a matter of emotion as well as analysis, I like to settle cases. It was that compulsion perhaps, as well as reasons which I cannot easily describe, which made me want to have litigants trust me, and then made litigants trust me. I was and am a natural-born settler of disputes, made even more determined by experience.

For example, in 1979, one of my colleagues on the Superior Court, Julius Title, had before him a divorce case. Not just any divorce case, but what was then the largest divorce case in terms of money that had ever been in the United States of America. Jack Kent Cooke and his wife were getting a divorce after more than thirty years of marriage. Cooke was the principal owner of the Washington Redskins; the Los Angeles Lakers; the Forum, a large indoor arena where the Lakers played, and many other assets. He was also the majority stockholder of a communications equipment company called TelePrompTer.

In other words, there was a great deal of money to be played with under California's community property method of dividing assets when a marriage breaks up. Naturally, since these assets were not piles of currency in a vault, there were different estimates of what the Cooke family holdings were worth.

For example, how do you assign a value to the Lakers? How do you value the Redskins? What is the value of the largest indoor sports facility in California? If Mr. Cooke wanted to hold onto these properties—which he did—he had to give Mrs. Cooke half of their value in cash. But how did anyone know what that value was?

A parade of appraisers, bankers, accountants, and lawyers had passed through Judge Title's chambers and courtroom for weeks and months, unable to come to agreement. Judge Title, a longtime friend, told me that if the parties could not settle, he was going to set it down for trial. He told me that the trial might well last for eight or nine weeks. But, he added, he would not be at all surprised if I could not settle it at all, considering the scope of the property and the complexity of the valuation.

A judge has pride just like a truck driver or a baker. Just because Judge Title had put it to me as a long shot, I was determined to make the parties settle. For two decades my clerks had referred to my aggressive efforts of settlement as "The Wapner Treatment." Now I was determined to apply the treatment to the Cooke divorce case. (Bear in mind, the Cookes, Jack and Barbara, had been divorced over a year earlier. We were attacking the hard part in 1979, the property settlement.)

For seven days, I heard the lawyers and their clients. I tried to acquaint myself with the facts—not down to the last detail of "depreciation" or "recapture" but in sufficient detail to render justice. I did not call witnesses, but I did ask the lawyers to tell me what the witnesses would have said had they been called.

On the eighth day, I told the parties that I was going to settle it that day. No one would be excused, and there would be no continuances (legalese for postponements). If a lawyer happened to have another appointment for that day, that was just too bad.

We started at eight in the morning. I talked to one side, then to the other side, then to the first side. I yelled and bullied and cajoled and urged. By noon, it looked impossible. So I pleaded with both sides to see reason. I argued. I explained. And, lo and behold, little by little, like a model airplane taking shape as a Spitfire when it had been just a pile of parts, the settlement appeared. At eight P.M. on the eighth day, we had a settlement that everyone could live with.

Jack Kent Cooke shook my hand. His ex-wife hugged me. They had a deal.

I am not going to try to rehash all the numbers and minutes of the Cooke settlement. It was at the time the largest divorce settlement any wife had ever received, in excess of $44 million. (Normally, I, like any other judge, would not reveal the terms of a settlement of this kind; however, the Cooke settlement has been in many newspapers and even in the *Guinness Book of World Records*.) But the point is not about the numbers but about trust. We were able to reach a settlement because the parties, Mr. and Mrs. Cooke, and the lawyers wanted to reach a settlement, and because they trusted me. Without that element of trust that I would help them arrive at a conclusion fair to each of them, the parties would have gone on to trial.

Now, please understand, I am not boasting that I am some kind of miracle worker, nor that I am a unique judge. I am saying that I worked terribly hard to earn the trust of people in the court system. Once I had earned that trust, I was able to save a tremendous amount of wear and tear on litigants by striving for settlements before trial. Because I had worked to merit trust, I could take some of the human cost out of the legal system. That was my goal, and often it worked.

The Cookes were so happy that Jack Kent Cooke invited me to be his guest at the Super Bowl the next year. The former Mrs. Cooke asked me to perform her wedding to her next husband—and I gladly did it.

To be sure, the Cookes could have afforded litigation. Their lawyers were perfectly capable of handling the litigation over property settlement in a conscientious, lawyerly way. At the end of the day, everyone involved would still have been among the living. The point is that it would have been wasteful of time, money, and the human spirit. That is what I wanted to avoid. I have always hated waste in all forms.

To me, litigation in civil cases is the last ditch, ultimate weapon, to be used only in cases of urgent necessity. It is so devastating in its consumption of everything precious in life that I will do almost anything to avoid it.

When I was in law school, way back in the stacks of the USC law library, there was a watercolor, sketched in England in the eighteenth century. It shows a milk cow. At one end, a man is pulling the cow toward him. He is labeled a plaintiff. At the tail is another man pulling the cow toward him. He is labeled defendant. In the middle, sitting on a three-legged stool, smilingly milking the cow, sits the lawyer.

This is too easy a swipe at lawyers and too much of a simplification of the process of lawsuits. Still, it makes a point. Litigation breaks and ruins all too many hopes and dreams if it proceeds to an ultimate, lengthy conclusion in court. Whenever it was possible, I tried my best to be a figure of trust, to step in and end the struggle so that everyone could go on to the most important things in life, which are definitely not civil lawsuits.

CHAPTER SEVENTEEN

Horse Sense

*U*nfortunately, not every try at settlement worked. . . .
Bill Davis, as I will call him, was a lawyer at a
prestigious law firm in Los Angeles's elegant Century City
business area. (This area is about half of a square mile of
high-rise office buildings and exclusive shops. It lies on
what was the back lot of Twentieth Century-Fox before Fox
sold it to a land developer almost twenty years ago, hence
the name "Century City.") There are many law firms
indeed in Century City, but among the most prestigious was
the firm of Hardy, Johnson, and Defoe, as I will call it,
where Bill Davis worked.

Davis was from a steelworkers' family in Pittsburgh,
Pennsylvania. He had worked his way up from virtually
nothing to be a senior associate at Hardy, Johnson, specializing in drawing up wills and trusts for some of the wealthy
people who live in Southern California. Davis made a good
living, with the prospect of much more to come. But he still
felt deeply insecure around the rich, and he was afraid that
he would someday be hindered by it.

The rich seemed to him to have a certain insouciant,
confident quality that he lacked. To Davis, they always

seemed to know how to get a table at a restaurant, how to order a decent bottle of wine, how to command respect, in a word. He felt that if he could only master that set of skills which marked the rich, he would be able to blend in better with them, do more work for them, become a partner at his firm, and generally be a more contented lawyer and human being.

His wife, who wanted to help, told him that she had read in a book about the English aristocracy that they, the English aristocrats, attributed much of their success in the world to their sureness in handling horses. If only Bill Davis could learn to ride a horse, he could surely, certainly, without question, become a more confident man overall, his wife suggested. Davis agreed at once.

By an incredible stroke of what seemed at the time to be good luck, no sooner had Davis made up his mind to be a successful horseman than one of his richest clients, whom I will call Pierre Dillard, invited Davis out to his ranch in Hidden Valley for the weekend.

Hidden Valley is a region of fabulous ranches and estates located in a valley just beyond the western end of the San Fernando Valley. In its precincts live some of the very wealthiest persons in the world, including the founder of Litton Industries, Roy Ash; David Murdock, a major corporate titan; and a number of plastic surgeons.

To Davis, this was his chance. His host, Pierre Dillard, told him that they would ride horses all day long on Saturday and Sunday. When Davis truthfully told him that he, Davis, had never ridden a horse, Dillard, a scion of a wealthy Kentucky family, said that would be no problem. "We'll just put y'all on a very quiet, sensitive horse that won't give y'all a moment's worry while we teach y'all how to ride."

Indeed, when Mr. Dillard started out to arrange horses for his guests (he later said in depositions), he fully intended to give Davis Martha, a ten-year-old, extremely contented bay mare. However, perhaps because he had enjoyed a number of Bloody Marys at breakfast, he got confused. He ordered his groom instead to give Bill Davis Trixie, a wildly spirited two-year-old Arabian. Trixie was so difficult to control that Pierre Dillard had just discussed selling her with his ranch manager two days before.

Totally unaware of the real nature of Trixie, Davis gamely got up on the beast and shifted in his saddle to make himself more comfortable. In so doing, he stuck his spurs—which Mr. Dillard had thoughtfully lent him—in the horse's flanks.

Trixie was off like a shot. She ran across the driveway, across a twenty-acre meadow, and then leapt across a flowing, picturesque creek. She made it to the other side. Bill Davis, LL.B., did not make it. He wound up dumped in the water, still wearing his elegant pinks, his neck fractured and himself paralyzed.

Mr. Davis sued, and I was assigned to judge the case. He alleged that Mr. Dillard had been grossly negligent in giving him such a dangerous animal to ride, especially as Dillard well knew of plaintiff's inexperience and had even promised him a tame and harmless horse. To have given such an inexperienced rider spurs in addition compounded the negligence, as Mr. Davis's lawyer said. Spurs applied to a frantic horse by a new rider are simply a way of begging for trouble, and now the trouble had to be paid for, as Mr. Davis's lawyer said.

Mr. Dillard raised a whole series of defenses through his litigation counsel, a whole different crew from those who had worked with Bill Davis before his resignation due to paralysis. Dillard said that first of all, Davis "assumed the risk" of injury by a horse by getting onto a horse. He was contributorily negligent, in other words. As Dillard's lawyer said, any man without horsemanship skills who gets onto a horse is assuming some risk. Further, Mr. Dillard's lawyer said, anyone who really wants to learn to ride should go to riding school. Mr. Davis could not have expected the same level of diligence from the ordinary host such as Dillard as he could have expected from a trained riding school. Mr. Dillard had been trying to be a good host to his lawyer, but he was not in the training business, and his level of care should not be required to be as high as that of a fully licensed and insured school.

As to the little matter of having a few Bloody Marys before sending Mr. Davis off on his horse, that was not more than usual Saturday-morning horse-riding etiquette, which might seem strange to city dwellers, but was really perfectly *de rigueur*.

The case went through depositions and expert witnesses were found and examined. I called the litigants into my chambers and spoke to them. Alas, Mr. Davis was still in his body cast and could not appear, but his lawyer, Stanley Van Zant, as I will call him, appeared. "I want this thing settled," I said. "It should never have come to trial in a million years. I want it out of here, and you two lawyers do whatever you can to settle it."

Within literally hours, the lawyers were back before me. Mr. Dillard's lawyer, "Martin Sanger," said he had an offer from his client and his client's insurance company. To end the litigation and dispose of all claims, they would pay Bill Davis the round sum of one million dollars.

This was in 1970, when a million dollars was a large settlement indeed. To this judge, who was then sending his son Fred to the University of California, Santa Barbara, and his son David to Berkeley, and his daughter Sarah to a private school, and was struggling to make ends meet, it seemed like real money indeed.

"I know that your client has suffered horribly," I said to Davis's attorney, Mr. Van Zant. "I know he is a well-paid man when he's healthy and that he has lost substantial income. But I also know that the prognosis is for complete recovery, and that he should be back at work within six months, his mental faculties unimpaired. I recommend this settlement."

Mr. Van Zant was indignant. "This is a drop in the bucket for the pain my client has gone through," he said. "It also fails to measure the callousness and contempt shown by the defendant to my client, with whom he had a relationship of trust. I cannot even pass this on to my client. He will be too hurt."

"Counsel," I said, "I suggest that it is your duty to pass that on to your client, and report back tomorrow morning with his answer. This case should be settled."

To my dismay, Mr. Van Zant told me and Mr. Sanger the very next morning that his client insisted on going through to litigation, and would not even consider the million-dollar settlement.

I thought it was a major mistake for Mr. Davis to be so stubborn, but under the rules of law, I could not even comment on the settlement as the case went to trial with Mr. Davis showing up for trial every day in his new brace and his wheelchair.

From the first day, things went badly for the plaintiff.

The defendant's lawyer, Martin Sanger, was able to show
Mr. Davis as a social-climbing buffoon who had simply
gotten in over his head in trying to be too rich, too fast. Mr.
Dillard came across as a courtly, kindly southern gentleman
who only wanted to be a good host and would no more have
purposefully harmed Bill Davis than shown disrespect for
Jefferson Davis.

The jury seemed to me to be listening carefully to the
medical descriptions of Mr. Davis's pain and suffering. But
they also listened carefully to Mrs. Davis's tales of how she
had hoped Mr. Davis could mix better with the rich if he
learned to ride. To the jurors, a group of retired secretaries,
nurses, and welders, as well as two housewives from the
East L.A. barrio, and an assortment of other good-and-true
men and women, Bill Davis simply did not come across as
a working class hero.

On the final day of testimony, Mr. Dillard had his stable
manager take the stand and in a sincere way say that no man
in history had ever been as respectful of either animal or
human life as Mr. Dillard. He told a long and involved story
about Mr. Dillard jumping into a bitterly cold lake in
Wyoming once to save a Cocker Spaniel puppy, and three
of the jurors had big tears in their eyes.

In the closing arguments, Mr. Van Zant gave a valiant
effort to make his client seem like a victim. He virtually tore
his hair out explaining how Bill Davis's life had been
wrecked by the savage Trixie, and by the gross negligence
of Pierre Dillard.

It was too late. The jury took only an hour and a half to
find that there was no legally actionable negligence on the
part of Mr. Pierre Dillard, and that whatever harm had come
to Bill Davis had come to him as a combination of bad luck,

his own incompetence and assumption of risk, and a small level of carelessness by Mr. Dillard which did not rise to the level of legally accountable negligence.

Bill Davis was hysterical, furious, outraged. He turned a hot scarlet in his neck brace and cast, making himself look almost like a cherry on top of a vanilla ice-cream cone. Later I saw him, his attorney, and Mr. Sanger in chambers to discuss certain housekeeping matters relative to liquidating the case. While Mr. Davis fumed, I could not restrain myself.

"Sir," I asked, "you're a lawyer. Didn't you have any idea that this would happen? Don't you know what a poor impression lawyers can make as witnesses?"

Mr. Davis looked at me plaintively and said, "Well, but they wouldn't even offer to settle."

"What do you mean, sir? I heard the defendant's lawyer offer a million dollars in settlement right here in my chambers before trial," I asked.

"A MILLION DOLLARS!" Bill Davis screamed. "I NEVER HEARD A WORD ABOUT THAT."

Mr. Van Zant turned to the wall and began to cough. "Uh, don't you remember?" he said. "I told you about that offer and you said to turn it down right away."

"I NEVER HEARD A WORD ABOUT ANY MILLION DOLLARS, YOU CREEP!" Bill Davis shrieked. "YOU BLEW A MILLION-DOLLAR SETTLEMENT OFFER? I'M GONNA KILL YOU!"

When the screaming died down, it was learned at least preliminarily that Mr. Bill Davis had never in any meaningful sense been told about the offer by his attorney, this from Mr. Davis and Mr. Van Zant respectively.

Certainly, it had never been communicated in writing by Mr. Van Zant to his client.

Now, you may think that this is a case about the total failure of settlement as a means of solving lawsuits. However, that would be wrong. The settlement was never given a chance. Mr. Dillard's offer was never communicated to Mr. Davis in any meaningful way. If it had been, the case probably would have been settled, a long lawsuit in court would have been avoided, and Bill Davis would have gotten something for his fractured neck besides a lesson in not trying to imitate the rich. If the essential element of communication had simply been added, the virtues of settlement would have been obvious. Even Mr. Dillard's insurer would not have come out that far behind, because he would have avoided the courtroom costs of the trial.

And, by the way, settlement did eventually preside. In the lawsuit for malpractice filed by Attorney Davis against Attorney Van Zant, the eventual result was a settlement for an amount I no longer recall, if I ever knew it.

My sons are both lawyers now. "Try to settle whenever you can," I tell them first of all. "Put anything important in writing," comes second. "Don't ever trust a horse named Trixie," comes third.

CHAPTER
EIGHTEEN

The Law of
Probability

*T*here can be other problems with settlement as well, which one might think of as "the lottery effect."

On November 15, 1969, which was my fiftieth birthday, a policeman named Joe Cipriano started a new job with the Los Angeles Police Department. He was going to leave the grimy, gritty world of cruising the streets in his black and white far behind, and take to the skyways. After eleven years as a traffic man, and then a vice man in the mid-Wilshire Division, Joe had paid his dues. He had taken a course in patrolling the city by night in a helicopter, and he couldn't wait.

First, he had gone to flying school at Van Nuys Airport. Then he had practiced with the craft above the sparsely populated northeastern end of the San Fernando Valley. Then he had flown as a passenger for a week with an experienced pilot and copilot. It was great.

No longer would he have to fight traffic on the San Diego Freeway, breathing in the fumes of trucks and buses. He would not have to worry about a drunken derelict attacking him as he waited at a stoplight. Instead, he would glide through the night sky, occasionally turning on his powerful spotlights to catch burglars or escaped convicts. As far as Joe Cipriano could tell, this was the first day of the rest of his life.

It was also very close to being the last day of his life.

No sooner had the turbines of his Bell CH-1 lifted him and his partner into the nighttime sky about the Ventura Freeway near the San Diego Freeway interchange than he heard an ominous rattle from the tail of his copter. His copilot also noticed the rattle, and turned so pale that he virtually glowed in the red lights of the cockpit. The copilot motioned to set the craft down in the nearby Sepulveda Basin. But the gesture was superfluous.

In a few seconds, the rotor went spinning off into freeway eternity, and the helicopter plunged to the freeway shoulder.

By a miracle, only one truck crashed into it, and by that time the copilot had dragged Joe Cipriano out of the helicopter anyway. In fact, Joe was barely conscious when he saw the copter go up in flames, causing a five-hour traffic backup on the Ventura and San Diego freeways, which is the next closest thing to a nuclear bomb falling on Dodger Stadium during the World Series.

At St. Joseph's Hospital, Joe Cipriano was diagnosed as not seriously injured. That meant he would walk again, but in the meantime would be in a cast for three months and in severe pain whenever he moved his arms for years to come.

He sued the LAPD and the maker of the helicopter. The maker of the helicopter said, "Who, us? We didn't do anything wrong. We were innocent. It was the bad guys at the Police Department hangar who didn't maintain the damned thing properly. The helicopter itself was perfect."

The LAPD said, "Hey, it's not our fault. The helicopter

was defective in a way which would not have been revealed by any kind of routine inspection."

The Police Department added that Cipriano should have known very well that the helicopter, any helicopter, needed extra special care in its rotors, and should not ever be taken up if there is any noise or unseemly vibration coming from those rotors. If anyone failed to do his job competently, said the LAPD, it was Cipriano himself. Therefore, he was contributorily negligent and should not be able to recover.

(It may surprise the ordinary citizen to learn that the LAPD was not more generous with its own man. Unfortunately, the tendency of employers whose employees are injured on the job is to place denial of liability above the claims of blood and loyalty. Even in the fraternity of policemen, money casts a spell.)

The case came before me on the Superior Court. As is usual, I talked to all of the lawyers for the different litigants and asked them what they expected to prove in court if the case went to trial. As you might expect, the plaintiff said he would prove that his client was severely injured through the negligence of the defendants. The defendants offered to prove that they were not negligent and that if there was negligence, it was largely on the part of the plaintiff for not examining the chopper carefully before he took off.

In addition, the defendants said they would challenge whether or not plaintiff was in fact severely injured as he claimed to be. They had experts, they said, who would say the results of the slow motion crash were not much worse than a bad fender bender on the street.

I urged both sides to settle. It seemed to me that plaintiff surely had a case, but not a case worth a lot of money. The defendants offered about forty thousand dollars. The plaintiffs turned it down, but I thought the case would still settle successfully.

Both parties disagreed, negotiations for settlement failed, and the case proceeded to trial. As the trial wore on, in the majestic courthouse at 111 Hill Street, I could not tell exactly how the jurors were reacting. Usually I have some idea of their leaning, but in this case I detected little sympathy for plaintiff or defendants in their poker faces.

Toward the end of the two-week trial, however, when defendants put on their medical witnesses, I thought that the jurors were impressed. Two different physicians, a man and a woman, both sincere and articulate, said that plaintiff would not have any lingering effects, and that with proper anti-inflammatory medication, even his painful shoulder swelling would soon go down and cause him little discomfort.

At that point, I noticed some agitation from plaintiff's counsel, as well as many whispered conferences between plaintiff and his counsel.

The attorneys made their closing arguments and summations. Then they waited while I charged the jury with instructions about negligence. But as soon as the jury retired, the plaintiff's attorney asked for a meeting in chambers.

At the meeting, the plaintiff and his lawyer said they had received a slightly higher offer from defendants and were inclined to take it. The new settlement was to be fifty thousand dollars. It was clear from the meeting that Cipriano was only reluctantly going along with his lawyer's advice and had wanted to await the jury's verdict until his lawyer had persuaded him otherwise.

But Cipriano nodded his head several times and said he

did want to settle for the fifty thousand dollars. I asked both parties on the record if they were agreeable to this latest offer of settlement. They said they were, and that was that.

We all marched back into the courtroom. A few minutes later, the jurors returned to tell us of their decision. The jury forewoman, a tall young redheaded model, cleared her throat.

"Madame, and members of the jury, I am bound to tell you that while you were deliberating, the lawyers in this case have reached a settlement," I announced.

The jurors looked distinctly downcast.

"I thank you on behalf of the litigants and the court for your time and effort. I am sure you did your best. But under the circumstances, the parties' agreement governs. I thank you all, and you are discharged."

The jurors filed out glumly from the courtroom into the hallway. Later, but only by moments, the lawyers for both sides went out into the hallway. One of defendants' lawyers began to banter with the redheaded model. In the course of making small talk, he made some large talk.

"Just between us," he said, "what was your verdict going to be?"

"We thought that Cipriano should get a quarter of a million dollars," she said.

By an unfortunate stroke of fate, the plaintiff himself was hobbling by at that very second. As I heard it, he started to tremble with rage and frustration. He ran after the juror to ask her if that was really true.

"Absolutely," she said. "We thought you deserved it."

In a flash, the plaintiff had collared his lawyer and was yelling at him about malpractice. "Look," the lawyer said to him after Cipriano had calmed down, "I'm getting paid a percentage of your recovery. Don't you think I would have liked to get a larger recovery, too? I was trying to help, trying to keep you from getting nothing. I saw the same reaction from the jury you saw. You agreed with me about the idea of settling.''

I have to sympathize with both the plaintiff and his lawyer in this case. Both of them lost out on getting a substantial sum of money. That has to hurt. Both of them have to feel that they were cheated, if only by themselves.

But Cipriano's lawyer was not being dishonest to his client. The lawyer really was seeking to take away the risk of getting nothing at all or almost nothing. He used his best judgment that perhaps contributory negligence would beat Cipriano down to a zero recovery. He was trying to do the sensible thing.

The tragedy is that word of what happened to Sergeant Cipriano seemed to get around like wildfire. All of a sudden, every litigant in California said to his lawyer, "Settle? Are you crazy? Think of what happened to that cop, Cipriano.''

But the truth is that what happened to Cipriano, barely missing a large jury award because he settled, almost never happens. The usual is that a settlement is at least as much as a jury would have awarded, taking into account legal fees. Plus, it is safe and secure. A settlement almost always is a good thing for both sides.

What happened in the Cipriano trial was the equivalent of a plaintiff winning a lottery. It was fascinating, but a prudent plaintiff does not count on it happening to him. To turn down a solid settlement because you think you might get a large jury verdict like the one in Cipriano (or other large cases) is like taking the grocery money to buy lottery tickets.

Jury verdicts are a lottery indeed in all too many cases. The virtue of settlement is that it takes away some measure of randomness and substitutes a measure of predictability. This is more of what I think law and the settlement of disputes should be about.

Yes, a jury can sometimes surprise a plaintiff. But happy surprises are much rarer than most people think. Settlements make sense in exactly the same way that buying a solid meal makes more sense than buying a lottery ticket. Few gamblers die rich, either at the track or in lawsuits. In life, as in law, compromise has a good name for a reason.

CHAPTER NINETEEN

Family Ties

Samuel Pincus (as I will call him) had been a hardworking man all of his life. He came to this country from Lithuania in 1933 when he was eleven years old, with his newly widowed mother. She died in transit of a cerebral hemorrhage. By the time Pincus arrived in Charleston, South Carolina—which was then a minor port of debarkation for immigrants—he was completely alone in the world.

Through the intercession of a nurse at the immigration facility, Pincus was sent to an orphanage in Petersburg, Texas, way out in the West Texas countryside, where there is little indeed on the landscape.

In the local Petersburg High School, young Pincus developed an extraordinary gift. He could do mathematical computations with amazing speed. He could also derive formulas for real world activities very quickly.

Not only that, but he could look at rocks and scrub and hills and gulleys and measure their size just with the naked eye.

In other words, Samuel Pincus, of a tiny town named Talus, in Lithuania, was a born oil and gas geologist. He spent three years at Southern Methodist University in Dallas studying geology, but he soon knew far more than most of his teachers. He graduated one year early, and within a year after graduation, he was a young rising star in the geology department of Humble Oil. The Second World War was raging, and his ability to find oil was so immense that he was deferred to seek that much-needed fluid.

In fact, he was sent by Humble Oil, with the full backing of the Department of War, to Venezuela to help local geologists discover what oil they could to add to their reserves near Lake Maracaibo. The details of his find are sketchy. But he helped the Humble Oil Company to find so much oil so quickly that he was put in charge of all South American exploration. By 1950, he had left Humble to start his own exploration and production company. He worked with larger companies to find oil and was rewarded with a percentage of the oil royalties from each field.

"Dr." Pincus (as he was respectfully called in Caracas) married a local woman, daughter of a Venezuelan geologist, Antonia Guzman. Together they had two children, a boy and a girl, named Raymondo and Patricia. The oil business went well until the early 1970s, then went incredibly well. By 1975, Pincus was a wealthy man. He moved with his wife, Antonia, and Raymondo and Pat to Holmby Hills, an extremely expensive area of West Los Angeles. In a great Spanish Colonial Revival mansion on Baroda Drive, behind a wall, with sloping lawns and lazily sprinkling water arcing above the hedges, Samuel Pincus planned to live out his life.

One year to the day after he settled into Holmby Hills, Mr. Pincus and Antonia went to visit a friend from Venezuela who was staying at the Santa Barbara Biltmore, in Montecito, right on the beach. Just as he was steering his

Cadillac Seville onto the Pacific Coast Highway in Oxnard, he suffered the same kind of cerebral hemorrhage his mother had experienced more than forty years before while she and her Samuel were crossing the Atlantic.

The Cadillac drifted into the next lane as Dr. Pincus lost consciousness and was literally crushed under an eighteen-wheel oil tanker heading from the Ojai fields to Taft, California, by a detour. Dr. and Mrs. Pincus were buried side by side at Garden of Rest Cemetery overlooking the San Diego Freeway two days later.

By the operation of Samuel and Antonia Pincus's will, all of the stock in Pincus Energy devolved upon Raymondo and Patricia, the only children. They were by then twenty-two and twenty-four. Each child received half of the stock of the corporation.

It was agreed in the teary reverie following the funeral that Raymondo, who was the older sibling, would run Pincus Energy while he was attending UCLA Law School. After all, Patricia was off to New York to become a junior editor at *Vogue*, and Raymondo was always more interested in money anyway.

Alas, talent for running a business is rarely inherited. Within three years, despite a uniquely large run-up in the price of oil occasioned by the Iranian revolution, Pincus Energy was losing money for the first time in its history.

Excess investment in a dry hole in the Amazon jungle, a defalcation by a new woman employee who had appeared to be such a nice person when Raymondo had met her, slow payments by local oil companies who were in a squeeze because so much of their assets were being siphoned off to the Middle East—all of these things combined with just plain inexperience to make Pincus Energy a less valuable company than it was when Samuel was running things. To Patricia's eyes, Pincus Energy was worth a helluva lot less than it would have been if she were in charge.

She demanded that Raymondo turn over control of Pincus Energy to her. She also demanded that if he did not do that, he simply sell the company to a larger exploration and development company while the getting was good.

Raymondo was affronted. He told her that women knew nothing about business anyway, and that operating Pincus Energy was much more difficult than she could even imagine.

After a few months of this byplay, the only communication between brother and sister was by mail.

Then the only communication was by lawyer.

Four years and three months after Pincus and his wife were crushed by that oil tanker truck, Patricia Pincus filed suit in Superior Court asking that her brother be removed from operational control of Pincus Energy, that a conservator of the assets be appointed, and that the firm be liquidated in an orderly manner.

The case came before yours truly as one of my final cases before I left the bench. Both sides were represented by extremely able counselors. Both sides had been told by their lawyers that the fight would be long and costly, and in the end might see them both substantially poorer than they were at the outset of the matter.

"I can't - - - - - - - forgive my brother for what he did to Dad's company," Patricia said through clenched teeth. "Go ahead with the litigation."

"That dope doesn't understand the first thing about the oil patch," Raymondo said. "I'll beat her brains out in court. Just wait and see."

For six months, incredibly expensive pretrial preparation took place. Both sides hired experts in the oil business. Both sides hired experts in management consulting. By the end of that first six months, I would have imagined that each side had spent a high-six-figure sum.

One day, when I was talking about trial dates with the lawyers for the brother and sister, the sister's counsel, a distinguished and longtime friend who had been on the Superior Court himself at one time, made a suggestion. "I know this is not usually done. But I would like for Your Honor to speak to the brother and sister yourself, in chambers, without either of the lawyers present. It's possible that when the lawyers are around, both sides feel as if they have to fight harder than they would if the lawyer were not around."

To his credit, the other counselor agreed. "It may be that neither side wants to appear weak in front of his counsel because we've spent so much time on this case. This might just be a time when the most direct possible approach is needed."

One week later, after Raymondo and Patricia had cleared their busy schedules, I saw them both in chambers at Superior Court Building at 111 Hill Street. Both were bright and attractive. They reminded me of my sons and my daughter Sarah. While they shifted uneasily in their seats, I tried to think of what would move them.

"Look," Patricia said, "let me start out by saying that this isn't just over money."

(It fascinates me that all cases which are about money turn out somehow to be *not* about money as soon as a third party is present.)

"What's it about, then?" I asked.

"It's about betrayal of trust," she hissed. "It's about a man who's my own flesh and blood and doesn't think I'm smart enough to have any say in the business. He's insulted me and he's insulted all women."

"I'm the one who's getting insulted," Raymondo, a dark, irritable, but articulate man answered. "I have been trying in a very difficult situation to keep Pincus Energy going smoothly. These worldwide energy distortions are impossible for anyone to follow. I have a lot of experts who'll say that I've done well considering the unpredictability of the marketplace."

"That's a lie," Patricia Pincus said. "Anyway, what he's done in the past is unforgivable."

I drew a deep breath and said, "All right, you two. I've heard enough." I said it in a loud, sharp voice and both brother and sister sat up in surprise. They had apparently expected a judge who would only go through the motions. "I am sick of hearing you talk about the past. Forget the past. Each of you did things that weren't perfect. But you two are your only close relatives in the whole world. You have to start thinking about the future. What's it going to be like to go through the rest of your lives being enemies with your only brother or your only sister? Who are you going to go to when you have a problem and only someone in your own family can help? What are you going to do when you're alone one night far away and you remember something about your parents that no one else ever knows about and you want to share it with someone, but you can't because you went through a trial and now you'll never speak to each other again?"

"But he took Dad's business and ran it into the ground," Patricia cried.

"The hell I did," Raymondo answered. "You don't know the first thing . . ."

"Look," I said very clearly. "I'm talking. I'm the judge. When I want you to talk I'll tell you. I'll agree that something should be done at Pincus Energy. Fine. We all agree. We can work it out here. Your lawyers can work it out. But you don't have to go through a trial to do that. You don't have to rip your hair out to get a shampoo. Trials are hard, painful processes. That's why they're called 'trials.' You go through this trial and I guarantee you that you'll hate each other for twenty years. Is it worth it? Is it so much more important to go to litigation than to settle that you'd risk your whole future as brother and sister? Is that how little your future means to you?"

I could see the brother and sister wavering. Instead of glaring at each other, they were now looking down modestly at the floor, one with her chin in her hand, one with his head in both hands.

"Six months ago," I said, "I had a case involving a quarrel between Robert Redford and two big producers about what movies he was going to make. He was smart enough to know that it doesn't pay to fight when you can settle. It doesn't pay to make permanent enemies in a small town like Hollywood because who knows when you're going to need the man you're fighting with today.

"If it's important not to make permanent enemies in Hollywood, how much more important is it to keep friends within your one and only family, especially now that it's shrunken down to just you two? Is it so impossible to compromise that you'll just toss away the closest tie there is and become strangers? I'm talking about your future, here. As brother and sister."

At that point, I could see that Patricia's face was clouding over with emotion. Raymondo's face was flushed. I drew my trump card and laid it on the table.

"If your father and mother could look down and see you two quarreling, clawing at each other, getting set to be enemies for the rest of your lives, how do you think they would feel? They would think that despite all the good they did, and all the respect they had in the world, their lives were a failure because they didn't bring you up with enough love to avoid this terrible fight. If your parents could look down from heaven at this lawsuit, they would cry. If they looked down and saw that you two had made up, they would smile and know they had been good parents after all, and that their lives were not in vain. Can't you settle this now? If not for yourselves, then for your parents?"

I had not even finished my speech before Raymondo and Patricia, in tears, were in each other's arms, swearing that they would settle, begging forgiveness, promising that they would respect the memory of their mother and father better from then on.

And to think that Mr. Kachel had been foolish enough to tell me I couldn't act. (By the way, the story about Robert Redford was true, and the only mistake in the settlement was that I settled it so fast that my wife didn't have time to come down to court to meet him. I heard about that later.)

But perhaps the reason I was able to throw myself into the case of the Pincus Energy heirs so artistically and with so much feeling was simply that I believed wholeheartedly in the result I was going after. This was not an acting audition to get into a senior class play—as important as that was. This was my real-life work to make a brother and sister save their lives.

In my deepest self, I was convinced of everything I told them, even if it was theatrical. Brothers and sisters who sue each other usually do spend years and decades not speaking to each other. They really do wreck their families. If there is any possible way to avoid ruining people's future lives by settling a case before trial, I will throw The Wapner Treatment at them as hard as I can. I did it when I was a judge on Superior Court and I do it now when I am a judge by order of reference.

Yes, the law will, if forced, take note of all kinds of disputes and if necessary take them through to litigation. But quarrels to the death in real life rarely help anyone, and litigation rarely leaves people in peace—although it does on occasion. *Settling* disputes is the best way to resolve them, as surely in court as in diplomacy between nations or within the smallest family.

If my peers from the Superior Court could say only one thing about me, I would hope it would be that Joe Wapner could feel other people's pain enough to know that settlement is a wonderful way to resolve a case. As I have said, I have seen what fighting leads to on Cebu.

CHAPTER TWENTY

Clear Thinking in a Muddled World

Since I have been on television and long before that, young men and women have been asking me what law school is like. Certainly to the young man at Georgia Tech or the young woman at Radcliffe, law school must be a mystery. The undergraduate sees the law student lugging around those heavy blue and red books. He sees law students haggard and pale from study while the undergraduates bask in the sunshine. What do law students do? he must ask himself, and then he asks me.

Law school is extremely different from undergraduate school. Law school has almost nothing—or at least very little—to do with memorizing facts. It has everything to do with understanding important contradictory concepts, lining them up alongside fact situations, and then seeing which legal concept governs.

Law school is about arguing, but not just arguing based on who can yell the loudest. Law school is about arguing based on universally agreed upon concepts and then seeing which competing concept is stronger in a given situation.

Law school—and law—is also about the changes which come into law as the result of changing attitudes in the larger American society generally, and how those changes can be integrated into an existing body of law without doing violence to the notion of law as a solid, dependable body of strictures upon which one can depend.

Or, to put this all into common sense and real life, take the case of Atchison, Topeka & Santa Fe, and how that famous railroad ran afoul of the People of the State of California.

In 1968, the district attorney in Los Angeles sued the Atchison, Topeka & Santa Fe Railroad under the California Health and Safety Code provisions relating to protecting the air we breathe here in Los Angeles, a dicey task at best.

Under the code, it was and is illegal for anyone to discharge thick black smoke into the air for longer than three minutes within any one-hour period. But the diesel locomotives of that railroad routinely had to burn diesel oil and emit thick black smoke for longer than five minutes. In fact, the railroad knew of no way to start up the diesel locomotives without burning that black smoke for longer than the allowable time.

Thus, if the state of California were to fine the railroad each and every time it started up a diesel locomotive, which is to say every time it violated the black smoke provisions of the Health Code, the railroad would simply be unable to haul freight into and out of California to the many different states of the American West.

The case came before me while I was sitting pro tem on the Court of Appeal. I heard the arguments and had to make the kind of decision law students have to make while writing papers or taking exams—or even answering in class.

On the one hand I had the agreeable principle that we all

want to keep the air in Los Angeles and California as fresh and pure as possible within the limits of the possible. Certainly no sensible man or woman could quarrel with that imperative.

Moreover, that imperative was now codified into law, so that it was absolutely clear that the will of the people of California was that to burn fires and generate thick black smoke was not to be countenanced by the people of California, at least not if the smoke went on for more than three minutes per hour.

On the other hand, the railroad was an ongoing business. Obviously, it was not a trivial enterprise either. Carrying produce and raw materials and manufactured goods in and out of California is an important value as well.

How does one reconcile these two needs, and if they cannot be reconciled, what principle may be employed to govern the need of a railroad to carry tomatoes and the need of a child to be able to draw a breath on Temple Avenue?

I studied a similar case involving a steamship which was also afoul of a clean air ordinance in New York City before World War II. In that case, the New York courts said that while both sides had clear and legitimate interests, it was quite certain that the state of New York lacked the power to prevent the great ocean liners from plying their routes between New York and the rest of the world. That power, over international and interstate commerce, belonged clearly to the federal government under the "commerce" clause of the Constitution.

To me, as well as to the two other Appeals Court judges on the panel, the exact same principle governed in the Atchison, Topeka & Santa Fe Case. If the state of California put a railroad out of business in California, it would be affecting and inhibiting interstate commerce in a big way. I wrote in my opinion's concluding paragraph, "We conclude, therefore, that the statute in question as applied to appellant herein under the circumstances shown by the record constitutes an unreasonable burden upon appellant's operations and as such substantially impedes the free flow of interstate commerce which is prohibited by the Constitution of the United States."

That is, the other judges and I resolved the perfectly good local interests and authorities of both sides by reference to the superior authority and power of the federal government.

The case of the smoking railroad locomotive is a little jewel of exactly the kind of legal complexity and lining up of different principles which is taught in law school. If thinking your way through fact situations like this one is exciting, maybe law school merits some thought for your future.

Then there are cases that involve changing attitudes in law and integrating them into the existing body of law, such as the case of *The People of California* v. *Mark Aranda et al.* Before I began to appear regularly on TV, my name was known to many law students largely for this case.

The case began in a sadly commonplace way. Two men, Henry Ruiz and Mark Aranda, were walking along the street in downtown Los Angeles when they decided to rob a jewelry store. Aranda, whose nickname was "Chop Chop," happened to have a pistol with him in a little case along with his after-shave and a length of rope.

The two men went into the Luna Jewelry Store and held the owner and a friend at gunpoint, then tied them up, and then ransacked the store.

About one week later, a suspicious policeman arrested both Aranda and Ruiz, who denied the crime. However, about one week after that, Ruiz apparently went into the police station and admitted the crime. "I did it, along with my pal Chop Chop," he said, or words to that effect. "The way you can tell is that the rope we tied the people up with smells sweet from the after-shave lotion that was in Chop Chop's case with it." After a moment's thought, Ruiz helpfully added, "Don't tell Aranda I told you."

The police disregarded this last request and instead charged both Aranda and Ruiz with armed robbery. I heard the case in 1963, one year after the alleged robbery. At the trial, the prosecution wanted to admit evidence of Ruiz's confession. Since there was almost no other evidence except an eyewitness identification which was no more than tentative, the confession was key to the state's case.

The defense counsel made an ingenious argument, which was not entirely novel. He said that the confession should be inadmissible because no matter what instructions I gave the jury, the jury would still take it as a confession not just by Ruiz, but also by Aranda.

After all, the confession had been that Chop Chop and Ruiz had done the robbery jointly.

But Chop Chop himself adamantly denied committing the crime. He had not in any way confessed. Thus the confession by Ruiz was in effect the involuntary confession by Chop Chop, and involuntary confessions are strictly prohibited by the Fifth Amendment to the Constitution which says that no one may be compelled to incriminate himself.

Thus, according to the capable defense counsel, I should not allow Ruiz's confession in the joint trial, since if it were allowed, it would immediately void the trial, as violating the defendant's Fifth Amendment rights.

The prosecution, on the other hand, said that the accepted rule was that when two defendants are being tried for a crime and one confesses, that confession may be introduced *if* the jury is instructed to disregard the confession as to the defendant or defendants who did not confess. The rationale was that it was often far more efficient to try all the defendants to a crime simultaneously. Also, the idea was that if you could not count on the jury to actually follow the judge's instructions and limit the effect of a confession to the defendant who actually confessed, then why have a jury system at all? If you cannot trust a jury to do what the judge tells them, the whole jury system is suspect.

So went the argument of the prosecution.

Again, both arguments were weighty, sensible arguments. We do not want people to incriminate themselves against their will. That is what the Constitution says, for good reason.

But we also do not want to have large numbers of trials for the same crime. We do not want to have the state forced to round up the same witnesses over and over again for one crime. The people have legitimate interests in an efficient system of prosecution.

This is a typical law school fact situation. In this case, however, it was happening in real life, and I had real flesh-and-blood men and women who had been robbed at gunpoint and real flesh-and-blood men who might have to lose their freedom depending on what I decided.

I considered the matter very carefully indeed. Already, by 1963, it was clear that the winds of change were blowing across the nation's criminal justice system. Just a few years before, the Supreme Court had ruled that all indigent defendants were required to have counsel. That had been a major departure from prior law. Now there were cases before the Supreme Court of the United States about many other areas of defendants' rights. It seemed certain that the shield of constitutional protection around defendants would be enlarged, and soon.

Still, I was trying the case in the here and now. My duty was to interpret the law as it was, and not as it might be at some future and highly conjectural date.

I admitted the confession into evidence with instructions to the jury to limit its effect to Ruiz and absolutely not apply it to Mark "Chop Chop" Aranda.

Both defendants were convicted.

Both appealed instantly, and in the two years that the case took to reach the Supreme Court of California the law had changed almost unrecognizably.

In the 1962 case of *Escobedo* v. *Illinois,* the Supreme Court had held that the state could not allow a confession into evidence *if* the defendant had not been told that he was a focus of the police inquiry into a crime, if he had not been told that he had the right to remain silent, and if he had not been told that he had the right to counsel paid for by either him or by the state.

The Supreme Court had, as many people predicted it would, expanded the shell of defendants' rights and greatly restricted police inquiries in the process. No longer could the police try to trick a confession out of a defendant by pretending they were after someone else. Nor could the police hold a suspect for a long period and deny him a lawyer. The state also had to warn suspects that they could refuse to answer any questions that might tend to incriminate them. (All of these rights were later put into a much more coherent form in the much better known *Miranda* decision.)

The decision was sweeping and was retroactive. Any convict who could show that his trial would likely have come out the other way had the newer court rules been in place at the time of his trial could get a new trial or an appeal based on the new Escobedo rules.

Now bear in mind something which is vitally important to the study of law. The *Escobedo* decision had fundamentally changed the way police could handle suspects. That same decision had been based upon a reading of the Constitution of the United States, especially the first seven amendments to the Constitution encoded in the Bill of Rights.

But the amendments on which the high court relied to make its changes had been put into the Constitution in approximately 1791! They had not been changed by a single word since then, although they had been applied to the states by the Fourteenth Amendment in 1868. So the laws which the Court was relying on to fundamentally change criminal procedure were at least a century and closer to two centuries old depending on how you look at it. The Congress and the states had not suddenly dropped a new sentence into the Constitution saying that defendants had to be read a list of rights including the right to have free counsel.

The Supreme Court justices had taken it upon themselves to expand the rights of defendants based upon their *interpretation* of the Constitution in the light of then current moods and trends. The mood of many of the leading legal commentators was toward a more generous interpretation of the Constitution as regards individual rights of defendants. That was put into law in the *Escobedo* and *Miranda* decisions (and many others) in the field of criminal procedure.

In the field of criminal procedure, a mood, a feeling of what was right, became law, pure and simple. Messrs. Mark "Chop Chop" Aranda and his pal Henry Ruiz went back into court, this time to the entire Supreme Court of California. Again, they protested that the confession of Ruiz should not have been allowed to be admitted into evidence because it tainted the case against Aranda, who had not confessed.

Through its able Chief Justice Roger Traynor, the California high court said that it had a great deal to say on the subject of confessions generally in criminal cases.

First, the court said that it did not even need to get into great detail on the issue of joint trials with single confessions because under *Escobedo*, not only should the Ruiz confession not have been admitted against Aranda, but should not have been admitted at all. Ruiz had not been advised that he could remain silent or could have counsel or was the focus of a specific criminal investigation. Hence, the confession obtained without those warnings was inadmissible, and thus the trial was fatally flawed by its admission, and the trial court, Wapner, J., was overruled. The decision was reversed for a new trial.

(That is, the defendants would not simply be allowed to go free as they do on "Miami Vice." They would be tried again without the admission of the confession. They might or might not go free after that trial.)

However, the California Supreme Court went much beyond *Escobedo*. They said that although it was not really necessary in the Aranda case, they would fashion a new set of rules for all cases involving two or more defendants and a confession by one or fewer than all.

The court said that a coerced confession was not simply

admitted with a warning to disregard it in American courts. Rather, it was deemed to be so prejudicial and influential toward a jury that it could not be admitted at all. By the same token, said the court, a confession by one defendant which implicates another defendant is likely to be so prejudicial that it also should not be admitted at all. It is, so Chief Justice Traynor said, simply another form of a coerced confession, this time "coerced" because made by one defendant without the other defendant having any voluntary input into whether it was made or not.

Therefore, from now on, if there was more than one defendant in a case, no single-party confessions could be introduced unless any and all references, no matter how slight, to the other defendants had been excised. If it was not possible for the prosecution to so edit the confession, then the trials of the defendants had to be severed. That was the new rule.

Now again, in *Escobedo* or *Miranda,* the justices were basing their ideas of criminal procedure on the U.S. Constitution and the California Constitution. But there had been no changes in either great document requiring any change in multidefendant trials. Rather, the justices were interpreting the cases in the light of a reinterpreted Constitution for the nation and the state.

I was reversed, and no judge that I know of likes to be reversed. But frankly, I believe the process of reinterpreting and reinvigorating the Constitution and every kind of legal procedure is so vital that I hardly mind at all being reversed in a case like Aranda. The Constitution is the finest work ever written, at least in my opinion, but it is a brief document, addressing only generally all of the areas of government. It cannot possibly have one answer for all eternity to each and every fact situation.

Like people, like societies generally, like this most superb country, the law must grow and adapt to needs and new conscience. After all, one hundred years ago, the Constitution was held to allow legally enforceable segregation by race. This was the doctrine of "separate but equal." That was the law of this country until I was thirty-five years old. Yet the nation became more humane and more enlightened, and the Constitution was reinterpreted to say that segregation by race was inherently unconstitutional on its face, despite any possible showing of ostensibly equal facilities.

At one time the Constitution of this country was held to allow compulsory internment of Japanese-American citizens. It is hard to imagine that it would be so interpreted today, even in wartime.

The law in this country lives, grows, breathes with the people of this country itself. Of course, we never want the law to change so as to change our basic freedoms or our living together in peace under law. But we do want a living Constitution, and we have one.

This, too, is what law school is like. Lawyers have to learn to adjust to an ever-changing body of law. They have to be able to work with the law as it is, and then work with it, to the benefit of their clients, when it changes.

Most sophisticated and pathbreaking of all, lawyers have to learn to use existing concepts and social notions to nudge a court into making new law when it is required. To take a grab bag of almost-related precedents, social imperatives, factual data, and historical truths and persuade a court to reinterpret the law rarely happens. But when it does happen, the lawyers who were in on it know that they were in on history in the making, and more to the point, law in the making.

How do you know if you would be good at law school and thereby good at law? Basically, you cannot know until you try it. Usually, you cannot know until you have tried it for a long time.

But . . . *if* you were the kind of kid who left his bat and glove lying where his father might trip over it on the path, and *if* he said to you, "Why on earth were you so dumb as to leave your bat and glove lying where I might well have broken my neck over it?" and *if you* said, "Well, Dad, I left it there not out of pure thoughtlessness or neglect, but because as a matter of principle, children should feel free to be casual, nonlinear, and even nonforesighted, and this will encourage my powers of imagination, and in the end make me a better citizen and a son you'll be proud of, . . ." if you can even say anything like that in a similar situation, you are a born-and-bred perfect lawyer.

If you are the kind of wife who, when her husband picks up a credit card bill and starts to hyperventilate, calmly says, "Look, I bought things that were either absolute necessities or which I, in the exercise of thoughtful consideration as an adult, decided I needed, and I bought them at a price which, considering the alternative uses of my time, was the best possible price I could have paid, good night," you should sign up for the law boards at once. Lawyers think up *good reasons* for why things should get done or did get done. That's their job.

What does it take to be a lawyer? Trustworthiness, persistence, responsibility, self-discipline, but most of all the ability to think in terms of concepts and to put concepts to work in factual situations.

Mentally, it is the hardest work I know of. But it is the center of everything that happens in society, and if you do it well, you do more than serve your clients: you serve the whole nation under the law. Law school is where you start.

CHAPTER TWENTY-ONE

A View from the Bench

Since you've stayed with me this far, I will let you in on a secret: Readers are by no means the only persons who learn from an author's book. The author probably learns more than almost any reader. Only after the author lays out all that he has to say can he truly understand for himself the significance of all that he has said. I have heard Supreme Court justices say that they sometimes do not know how they feel about a case until they write the opinion and reason it out in writing. Certainly, as a judge, I often felt the same way. I often did not know how I would decide a case or a motion until I began to lay out the facts and the reasoning on a pad or more formally. By the exact same logic, an author often does not know precisely what the conclusions of his book will be until he has finished.

The fact situations, arguments, and momentum of a book are only fully apparent even to the author after they are laid down for his or her thought.

As a judge on Superior Court, I would never have felt as if I could fairly render a verdict in advance of hearing the evidence. Now, as an author, the evidence I have marshaled from my two decades on the bench is in, on paper for me to analyze just as you have in reading the cases and anecdotes here.

As it turns out, this is one of those happy cases where the evidence seems to me to merit an extremely positive verdict, a judgment that, with flaws and exceptions, the view from the bench is an encouraging vista indeed.

If this were a criminal trial about whether the legal system as I have seen it is guilty or not guilty of failing to render justice, I would absolutely have to answer "not guilty," and direct a verdict of acquittal.

If this were a civil trial in which society-at-large had accused the judicial system of failing to work for the benefit of justice and the ordinary citizen, I would have to answer that the case has not been made, and find a verdict for the defendant legal system.

Now, to be sure, my view from the bench has by no means been all sweetness and light, roses and evening flowery scents along the seashore. But it has been *on balance* encouraging indeed for me to review the way the legal system has worked in the cases in which I have been involved.

The failures that I have seen in the legal system generally come under a few quite specific headings.

First, the jury system is a highly imperfect system. Trial by a jury of one's peers all too often means trial by persons who can fall for melodramatics and lawyers' displays of hortatory fireworks. Sometimes it means a juror who refuses to see any logic or fact in a case, and instead sees that a defendant reminds him of his son or his daughter, and therefore absolutely resists finding fault. In my career on the bench, I have seen a few too many cases in which the facts were just not understood rightly by a jury or by one or a few members of a jury, and justice therefore did not prevail.

The problem is that there is just no alternative to a jury system that is superior to it. The idea that ordinary men and women will be judged by other ordinary men and women and not by the henchmen or satraps of the monarch was a brilliant idea in English law. It is still a good idea even when judges are civil servants beholden (I hope) to no one and no ideology except justice. We as a society are so deeply committed to the ordinary citizen having the last word in politics, consumer decisions, and law, that the jury system is here to stay.

When the jury system fails to see justice the same way a judge sees it—and make no mistake, this does happen—the price paid is a small one compared with keeping the fate of the citizen-defendant in the hands of other citizens. I wish jurors took their responsibilities more seriously at times, but in the great majority of cases, they discharge their responsibilities carefully.

I am concerned on a continuing basis about the respect of law enforcement officials for the law. By a vast margin, policemen and policewomen want justice and fairness as much as any judge. But there are still some who see their role as to "get" the bad guy, and see any law or procedure or Constitution that stands in their way as a needless obstruction to be gotten around and avoided. The policeman who claimed to see through a keyhole what he could not possibly have seen, the traffic cop who said there was a stop sign where there was none, are definite problems in the law enforcement mechanism. But they are incidental to the fine enforcement of law and respect for justice I usually witnessed.

Sadly, there are those, even in very high places in the

society, who also apparently see basic protections of the Bill of Rights as an unnecessary inconvenience in the fight against crime. It would be valuable if those men and women could see the need for the protections of law—even when those protections surround suspects in crimes. Perhaps there needs to be a refresher course for all police officers, judges, and attorneys general about why protections against illegal search and seizure, enforced self-incrimination, and deprivation of legal counsel are basic to the legal guardianship of all the citizens of the country.

We are a free people largely because we have a great many legal rights surrounding each and every man and woman in the society. If we start picking away at those rights because we fear muggers and robbers, we will be endangering our society a great deal more than any number of robbers and muggers could. No self-respecting people ever lost their freedom because of street crime, as horrible as that crime is. Nations lose their freedom when they lose the protection of the law.

I hope that the whole nation begins to see that as clearly as those of us on the bench do. Frankly, I believe that most Americans already know the value of law, and it is only a handful everywhere who fail to respect the safety it provides to every one of us.

As a judge, I was occasionally disappointed by the antics of lawyers. In my view, lawyers are supposed to adhere to an extremely high standard of conduct. They are officers of the court in both word and fact, as I see it. They have a responsibility to behave ethically and lawfully in whatever representation they have. When I saw them abusing the trust of their clients and the time and patience of the court, I was deeply disturbed.

Lawyers are given a place of privilege in this society. They are allowed to toil in the majestic edifice of law. This provides them with dignity, challenging work, social power—and often an excellent income. For those privileges, the least they can do is behave with respect toward the institution that gives meaning to their lives: the law.

Perhaps most of all, my vista from the bench has been marred by the sight of the unwinding of the threads that bind men and women together into families, neighborhoods, and a nation.

By definition, a judge sees people when they are in conflict. But over the last twenty-five years, I have seen more conflict than I used to, and far more than is healthful. Men and women seem to have lost a certain amount of ability to resolve their problems by themselves. Somehow, they have lost sight of whatever binds them to each other, and see only what separates them.

I saw neighbors who had not spoken in ten years, families who did not even know where their children were from year to year, business associates who thought that stealing from one another was routine. I saw a steady erosion of almost all of the best values that the word "community" calls to mind.

In the place of trust and good feeling and a spirit of sharing and compromise, I saw far too much resort to the courts to settle grievances.

This overreliance on the law courts and the failure of the person-to-person feeling that it represents were and are deeply discouraging to me. Law is supposed to be a last resort when neighbors cannot work things out themselves. It is not supposed to be a replacement for a decent regard for one's fellow human beings.

In a sense, this failure of community made me the saddest of any of what I saw on the bench. I fear that it marks a social deterioration beyond the power of any court to correct. If correction there is to be, it will have to come from a movement of human beings themselves, from the inside out, so to speak. To me, this is deeply important and bears considerable further address.

But all of these flaws are eddies and backwaters in what I see as a general ongoing flow of progress, growth, and strength in American law. The jury system is still strong. Our police are superb. In most cases, lawyers are competent and dedicated. Those who would abandon the ship of the Constitution when the waters of crime get choppy are in the distinct minority everywhere. The loss of community is not by any means universal, and I believe it is within the power of the American man and woman to reverse it and rebuild communities.

In the twenty years I spent on the bench, I saw overwhelmingly men and women who believed in the sanctity of the law. Before me every day came people from trash collectors to civil servants to corporate titans, and all of them were unified by trust in the law.

When the law recognized that the names on the dockets belonged to people, flesh and blood men and women who felt pain just as every other kind of person, the law worked miracles. What the law could do for the woman who had unintentionally not paid a street assessment and was about to lose her home was a wonder. I was proud to be the instrument of justice in the case. When I saw the young man from Alabama, Johnny Archer, and then watched the jurors not only acquit him but raise money for him to go home on a bus, I was touched indeed with what the law—through individual human beings—could feel. A brother and sister came into my chambers fuming with rage with one another. They left embracing. The law, through a judge who knows that the law is about people, was able to bring about a reconciliation in the blood.

In my years on the bench, I have seen that the law as an instrument can be flexible, subtle, understanding, and kind—even as, if need be, it can be exacting, harsh, and severe. I have seen this versatility in the law, and I have been a moving force in it within my own courtroom and chambers.

I do not mean to brag about this: the glory does not accrue to Joe Wapner for what he did in one court in one city. The glory is that the American law can accommodate the pain of the people before it, the concern of thousands of judges who can feel that pain, and then, far more often than not, render justice.

The crowning achievement is that as of the year I am writing this, the nation is marking two hundred years under its Constitution, making us the most long-lived nation in the world under the same written governing law. And this success is compounded by the surprising fact that Americans today actually enjoy far more protection of the laws than they did in 1787. The law as a system of protecting the innocent, punishing the guilty, and regulating men's affairs with justice is far greater and stronger than it was in the days of Jefferson, Madison, and Adams.

Yes, there are terrible problems in this country. Yes, life is always hard, even for the best of men and women in the best of times. Certainly, there is much to be done always and everywhere in law and in personal relations. (I will mention some of my own solutions in the Afterword.)

But for Joe Wapner, who started out planning to be an actor, who barely made it alive out of a crossfire on an obscure Philippine island, to have been for twenty years a feeling, moving part of the most magnificent structure of laws in the history of mankind, to have played a role in feeling and healing pain, in dispensing justice to the afflicted, was pure honor. There cannot have been a more fulfilling way to have spent most of my adult life. The view from the bench was—and is—spectacular indeed.

AFTERWORD

*T*he most haunting of life's mysteries is that time, which seems so permanent at the moment, passes and is gone. I have never quite acclimated myself to that basic truth. I fight against it in all kinds of different ways. For one thing, I try to remember the people and events of the past and keep them from fading into nothingness. My grandparents are no longer living as most people understand that word, but they live vividly in my memory each day. Some of the young men who came ashore with me on Cebu came back from there in a box, but they, too, are living in my mind.

For another thing, I make a point of staying close to the people who made up my past, and make certain that they are also a large part of my present.

For yet another, I try to make some sense of what has happened. It would be unbearable for me to think that it was all a mad, meaningless rush of events and accidents, without any residue of lessons and guidance to prepare me and others for the future. For example, it has been fifty-three years now since I graduated from Virgil Junior High School. When I graduated, in 1934, it was the lowest depth of the Great Depression. I know that there have been severe economic downturns since then, but the Great Depression was uniquely painful. Across the country, in 1934, more than 20 percent of the *breadwinners* in all American families were without jobs. That meant that one family in five had no private means of support, a figure never even approached since then.

But when I was at Virgil, I was twelve, thirteen, and fourteen years old. I knew nothing about the national economy or about statistics. I did see that nobody had much money and that what little you had should be saved. For that small bit of wisdom, and because I had tried to be a friend to all in my school, I was made chairman of the Virgil Junior High School Thrift Committee for 1933–1934.

To be sure, this was a minute event in a human history. But for me, it was large indeed. It was my first brush with responsibility outside the home. Encouraging my classmates to save, then and now, meant a great deal to me, even if they were saving pennies. To this day, I still go to each and every year's reunion of my class from Virgil. Time has thinned our ranks, so now we bring a few "kids" from the classes of 1933 and 1935 to our gatherings, and I always am glad I went.

Something good happened back there. I knew some fine people. I want to hang onto that as long as I can.

On my first day as an undergraduate at the University of Southern California, I met Art Manella. He was a junior when I was a sophomore. He was friendly and outgoing with me from the word go. He was at the top of his class academically and head of his fraternity, but he was never too busy to help me, a lowly freshman. Art's father had a grocery store at Vernon and Budlong, near USC. Art often worked there after class in his gray linen smock, as grocery store employees used to wear. I still vividly recall going to that store and sitting at the long fountain while Art helped me to fill out the application forms for a New Deal National Youth Administration job on campus. To my freshman eyes, he was the embodiment of what college and learning were all about. I was a philosophy major in college, and I recall how I used to see Art studying in the philosophy library day and night because it was the quietest place to study. He was always solicitous, and like a big brother to me.

After college, Art went on to be number one in his class at USC Law School. Then he went to Harvard Law School and earned a master's degree in taxation. He started a law firm which has become one of the most successful firms in Los Angeles and as a matter of fact in the whole country.

It has been fifty years since I met Art Manella at USC. But in that time, he has been the same kind, true friend that he was on the first day I saw him. Even at his peaks in school and in his career—and he still has many more summits to attain—it has never been in his nature to play big shot with me or anyone else. I have for the last five decades routinely asked him for help whenever and wherever I needed thoughtful, concerned advice about any important turn in my life. Of course I did not ask him how to decide cases, but in my personal life his counsel was indispensable and always there.

On the first day of law school in 1945, on November 1, I walked haltingly up the steps to the USC Law School. Only the day before had I gotten off my crutches and left the hospital where I had been sent by a Japanese gunner. There on the steps of the law school I saw two of my former undergrad classmates, Gordon Wright and James Hastings. We talked for a while about the war. I found out that by one of those coincidences of fate, Gordon Wright had been a lieutenant commander on a destroyer shelling Cebu before we landed in that horrible week in April 1945. Jim Hastings had been a captain in the Navy. We reminisced about absent friends, and then we went into our torts class.

Almost immediately, we established a pattern. After classes ended at noon on Friday, we would gather in a small room in the library, far underground. We would eat our brown-bag lunches. Then we would discuss each and every case the professors had covered that week. We would agree on what the rule of law was for each case. Then we would take turns at a typewriter, making three carbon sets of notes with summaries of the cases and the rules of decision of each case. We used these notes to study for the final exams and then for the California Bar.

Making our summaries and then discussing them took more than all of Friday afternoon. At around six P.M. each Friday we would take a break, walk across campus, and have dinner at Carl's Restaurant. Almost every time, we would begin with a martini, which cost fifty cents, and then have the spaghetti dinner, which cost ninety-five cents. It was the most any of us could afford. That was forty years ago, and I still recall as I write this how delicious that tomato sauce and pasta tasted after a hard afternoon studying causation and chains of title and res judicata versus collateral estoppel. The most expensive, most time-consuming meal at any French restaurant today cannot compare.

After dinner, we would return to the library and finish up our notes at about eleven P.M., completely and utterly exhausted, but happy.

Jim Hastings and I were both ushers at Gordon Wright's wedding. All three of us used to study for finals at Jim's house in Pasadena. I still recall how his son, Gary, who was three at the time, would run through the house, playing and yelling cheerfully. Now that son, Gary Hastings, is a Superior Court judge. I went to his swearing-in ceremony. Gordon's sons are both successful lawyers. I performed the wedding for one of them.

Gordon Wright is a senior partner with a major Los Angeles law firm, Lillick, McHose & Charles. Jim Hastings is a Justice of the California Court of Appeals. I talk to them with great regularity. We share our lives today, our memories, and keep alive the camaraderie of those days.

When I first began to practice law, my very first client was a man named Harry Leddel. Harry had been an optometrist but became a jeweler. He needed representation, and I needed a client. I had known his wife at USC even before I met him. I apparently did a decent job for him, and in return, he and his wife fixed me up with the blind date who turned out to be Mickey, my wife and life's companion.

Mickey and I are still extremely close friends with the Leddels. Even if we go two months without talking, when we do get together we pick up the threads of our lives without a moment's lapse. Their son is in business with his father. He uses my son Dave as his lawyer.

I am trying to make a simple point here, only it keeps turning out not to be so simple. Life is brief, confusing, and frequently painful. In my life, I have seen the sweetest, most innocent young men horribly maimed and killed utterly without reason except that they were in the wrong place at the wrong time. When I was a judge on Superior Court, I saw horrifying things. A man was jilted by his wife and then killed her to make her love him! Small children were run down after a happy day of play. Men and women went into hospitals in good health and came out permanently crippled. Helicopters crashed into the highway. Fathers died and children fought. Misguided men and women planted bombs and blew up totally innocent passersby.

The law could attempt to make things right, and did its best. The law could try to impose some order, and often succeeded. But life itself remained, and always will remain, bewildering, frightening, and unpredictable, in far too many instances.

To the extent that there is any remedy at all, I have found it in loyalty and friendship.

This is the key lesson I have drawn from the rush of events that make up "the past."

Life is too powerful to face alone. Even in America, the best of nations, even in the age of antibiotics and air-conditioning and automobiles and affluence for tens of millions, life is capricious and overwhelming. No one, not a judge, not a general, not a president, can face it alone. The famous French writer, Jean-Paul Sartre, said that man could not live successfully without commitment. I agree, and I believe that the commitment must be to other human beings and to human feelings and values. When one is lucky enough to get the commitment of other human beings in return, that is about the maximum reward that can be found in life.

That is—as I have tried to say in these small histories—in law, the human touch is everything. That ability to feel other people's pain, to put myself in their shoes and try to ease their suffering, is crucial to the satisfactory working out of legal conflicts.

But more than just in the arena of law, the link between man and man, between man and woman, between woman and woman, is what redeems life. The connection of one traveler on this planet with another is key to making life possible, and more than that, meaningful.

In a social context, friendship and loyalty means connecting up meaningfully with the men and women around you. Friendship and loyalty signify that you have a responsibility to other people, neighbors, friends, colleagues, citizens, and that they have a reciprocal duty to you. At its best in a social situation, by which I mean everything from a workplace or a school to a nation, friendship and loyalty as deep-seated values mean that you owe an obligation to behave with respect and care and concern toward the people who need you and respect you. In today's world of "me first and devil take the hindmost," for far too many people, those simple values, friendship and loyalty, are too often more honored in the breach than in the observance. But whatever happiness and feelings of contentment have come my way have come largely from those simple words: friendship and loyalty.

After I graduated from law school, I had to take the California Bar, as every other man or woman who wants to practice in California does. The Bar is an examination testing fairly detailed knowledge of the law of the state and nation in many different areas such as family law, torts, property, and contracts. Its function is to ensure a minimum level of competence among practitioners of law in California. It is justly famed as one of the most difficult Bar exams in the nation.

While I was studying for the bar, my wife befriended a woman whom I will call Lorraine Monroe. Lorraine was married to a bright young fellow whom I will call Bob, who had just graduated from UCLA Medical School and was interning at UCLA hospital. One day in 1948, Lorraine had to take Bob to a doctor in Beverly Hills. While she backed into a parking space, she accidentally hit a parked motorcycle. There was no damage to the motorcycle, and Bob went on to his appointment.

A vengeful passerby, however, reported the incident to the police, and Lorraine—who was pregnant at the time—was cited for misdemeanor hit and run. She was terrified, certain that her child would be born in jail. She asked me to help her with the charge. I had not yet passed the Bar, but my father, a capable trial lawyer indeed, kindly represented Lorraine at trial. He pleaded her guilty and then spoke to the court on her behalf. She was given a $15 ticket and a small time on probation. She was not back in court again.

From the moment of the accident on, we were fast friends. The Monroes had three lovely children, two boys, Andrew and Mitchell, and a girl, Karen. They were friends of our kids, and we all knew whatever was to be shared in each other's lives.

In 1957, Karen started to complain of headaches and nausea. Her father Bob, by then a successful young physician, had her examined at once. Catastrophe. She was diagnosed as having an inoperable tumor of the brain stem. By the most drastic measures of medicine, she lived for two more years.

She was a beautiful child, with long brown hair and a ready smile. Even when her hair came out from her treatment, even when she was thin and gaunt, she had a ready laugh for visitors. I made it a practice as often as I could, which was several days a week, to leave my office early and come by to visit her. We would play cards or make nonsense jokes or just sit together and watch television. She died in 1959, an innocent flower, taken before she had even begun to open to life's possibilities.

Mickey and I sat with Lorraine and Bob as often as they would have us. So did the rest of our circle of friends. No one ever had to ask us, and no one ever had to say "thank you."

In 1965, Mitchell, the middle child, started to have trouble remembering. He was a high-school student and had always been at the top of his class. Now he could barely do his work. At first he was diagnosed as having psychological problems, perhaps severe anxiety. He was sent to a psychiatrist, but the lapses got worse. A neurologist was consulted, and again, there was catastrophe.

Mitchell was diagnosed as having an inoperable tumor of the brain, on the cerebral cortex. The boy had about two years of radiation, and then he died. Once again, Mickey and I and our friends sat with Lorraine and Bob for as long as they would have us around. Sometimes for hours on end we would simply sit and say nothing, just to offer company.

Incredibly, the older son, Andrew, fell ill in 1970. He was only twenty-two, an excellent student at the law school of the University of California at Berkeley, engaged to marry a lovely woman who went to school with him. After a few tests, the next act of tragedy unfolded: Andrew had an

aggressive form of leukemia. He was given, at most, two
years to live.

He came back to Los Angeles for his treatment. As you
might imagine, his father and mother were tormented and
frustrated beyond words. Bob Monroe himself was an
extremely capable medical man. Yet he and Lorraine could
basically do nothing but watch and hope as their children
died by degrees before their eyes. Lorraine and Bob were in
relentless anguish.

Still, Andrew Monroe kept up an almost superhuman
bravery. He never complained, was always the liveliest in
any gathering until the very end. Several times a week,
when his treatment had just begun, I went over to his home
and played bridge with him. The teams would be our mutual
friend, Herbert Hill, who was my friend and contemporary,
and yours truly against Andrew and his closest friend, Harry
Chotiner. Despite his illness, his treatment, despite everything, he was still a formidable player. We would go at it
with no holds barred, swearing as we lost tricks or contracts,
and screaming if we made them. The young man had guts
beyond what I would have thought conceivable.

His fiancée insisted that they go through with their wedding and then go for a honeymoon in Europe. Then, a few
months after their return, after many more rubbers of bridge,
after carrying on over hearts and trumps, Andrew, too, died.

Again, our circle drew around Lorraine and Bob. No one
ever had to ask or suggest. No one ever had to say anything.
It was understood without words that their grief was our
grief and our strength was theirs.

Lorraine and Bob loved children. They decided to adopt.
Through a lawyer here, they found a birth mother who
wanted to give up her child. They took her child, a

daughter, into their home as soon as she was born, and immediately into their hearts as well. But California law allows a birth mother to change her mind up to six months after turning her baby over to the adoptive parents. Astoundingly, after three months, the birth mother came and took the baby away.

Bob and Lorraine Monroe had to watch in agony as a child they loved was wrenched from their arms and taken away forever. Again, Mickey and I sat with them as long as they needed us, and so did our other friends. In every sense, Lorraine and Bob were getting no more than they deserved. Every moment of need that Mickey and I had ever faced had seen them here without our even having to ask. It was simply automatic that we would be there for them as they had been for us.

I do not want to give the impression that the themes of loyalty and friendship were played only to the background sounds of tears or to the emotional counterpoint of tragedy. Mickey and I can and often do recall the couples for whom we played matchmaker—especially when we knew better than either the future husband or wife that they were right for each other, and stuck on the job to make sure that the wedding bells sounded. There have been children of friends whom we helped through school by example and encouragement, young men and women whose first jobs we helped to get, confused friends at any age with whom we counseled and then watched them triumph at life. The touch of a hand, the opening of a heart, are gestures which are made in times of gain as well as loss.

Nor have our acts and feelings been unilateral within our circle of friends. Friendships and loyalty have traveled a two-way street to the Wapner home.

In late 1969, I was elected presiding judge of the Los Angeles Superior Court. The job of executive officer of the court was vacant. We needed a top-notch manager in the job. I appointed a selection committee of three judges to start examining candidates for the job. By the rules of the selection committee, at least two of the members of that committee had to vote for a candidate to place him or her before the executive committee for the final choice.

I got a recommendation from an associate justice of the California Supreme Court that I talk to a young man named Frank Zolin. After I spent an afternoon talking to him, I was sure he was right for the job. But he got only one vote on the selection committee, which was not enough to get him before the executive committee.

My solution was simple. I managed to get the selection committee procedure democratized so that one vote was sufficient to get a candidate to the executive committee. Frank completely justified my faith in him when he appeared before the executive committee, which rapidly and over-whelmingly chose him for the job.

Several years later, Frank and I went to a conference on judicial administration in Snowmass, Colorado, one of the truly beautiful spots on earth, in a valley in the Rockies, quite close to the famous resort of Aspen. One day, a group of us went out into the forest to hike and fish. Frank was casting his line through the day, enjoying the wilderness and the change from Los Angeles, and then left with the rest of us for dinner.

Abruptly, he touched his finger to his other hand, then said he had to run back to the fishing creek. He disappeared for a couple of hours. When he returned, he seemed relieved. I later learned that while fishing he had inadvertently lost a signet ring I had given him to mark his fine work on the court. It was not a lavish ring, certainly not from Tiffany, certainly not the possession or the gift of a wealthy man. But I was touched that the small symbol of my faith in him and his living up to it had meant so much to him. His going back to find that ring—miraculously enough, still on the bottom of a clear, swift-running creek—means far more to me than any material thing. It means that a fine public servant acknowledged my gratitude and friendship and trust and returned it in kind. I am off the Superior Court now, but I still stay in close touch with Frank, and expect to for the rest of my life.

Friendship and loyalty. When I was on the Superior Court, my name was repeatedly suggested to the governor for an appointment to the California Court of Appeals. In fact, I served on that court pro tem for a year in the late 1960s, which is where I tried the cases about the "holy fathers" and their explosives, the locomotive engines pounding out black soot, and other cases. But I never got that appointment.

The appointment of judges in California is at the governor's pleasure. It usually pleases him to appoint people who agree with him. I had a bad habit of fighting back against assaults on the judiciary by the executive branch. That does not give governors pleasure.

In 1975 and 1976, I was head of the California Judges' Association. California at that time had as its governor an unusual young man named Edmund G. "Jerry" Brown, Jr. He had a number of idiosyncratic ideas. Among them was the notion that judges in California did not work hard enough and therefore should have their pay reduced. (He also had the interesting idea, which he apparently got from Mao Tse-tung, that all civil servants should make the same amount of money, so that a chief surgeon at a municipal hospital, for example, would make as much as a gardener.)

From my personal perspective, these were foolish notions. As a matter of the basic facts of life, it is hard enough to get decent judges to come on the bench at any time. Successful, hardworking lawyers can earn far more in private practice than they can on the bench. The difference can be a factor of ten. Of course, a sincere commitment to the public welfare and to public service evens out the odds somewhat, but judges are men and women just like other men and women. They need to pay their bills, raise their families, and provide for their children. The idea that the state of California could get judges as good as it needed with a drastic pay cut was simply wrong.

As head of the "union" of Superior Court judges in California, I was not going to let anyone, even the governor, belittle the work that judges were doing and get away with claiming that judges were overpaid.

I spoke out as forcefully as I could at meetings and conferences, in letters to the editor and guest editorials, and in testimony before the state legislature, and said that in my opinion, California's judges were not loafers sponging off the public till. Rather, they worked extremely hard for relatively modest pay, largely out of devotion to the public good. (Bill Munnell, a longtime friend and classmate from USC Law School, former majority leader of the State Assembly, then a colleague on the Superior Court, was often at my side, agreeing with me. Friendship and loyalty, reciprocal and repeated.)

This got me in hot water with the governor and his aides. As it was reported back to me at the time and later, when my name was brought up to be an appellate judge, Jerry Brown and his aides recalled the basic disagreements I had with the governor. The nomination never took place.

I will not pretend that it did not hurt. It hurt a great deal, and not because I was desperate to go onto the Court of Appeals. Frankly, I have always preferred the work of a trial judge. Rather, I was saddened that in America, a man's career can be stymied because he speaks out for the honor and reputation of his colleagues.

What I had done to defend the judges of California was a small and very well deserved measure of friendship and loyalty for my fellow judges. In return, the judges of California showed me in a hundred small ways and large that they appreciated it and reciprocated the feeling. Our close friends always let us know that Joseph A. Wapner on the Superior Court meant as much to them, and not a bit less, than if he were on the Supreme Court.

To the people we had gone on double dates with, played tennis with, laughed and cried with, studied with, grieved and triumphed with, my station in their eyes was not determined by how many lines I had in *Who's Who*. It was judged by my friendship and loyalty to them, and that, I hope, was always at the highest possible level. I would never knowingly allow it to be otherwise.

The histories with Lorraine and Bob Monroe, with the Leddels, with couples whose marriages we encouraged, with all of our friends, are of course small things in the context of the great world. They are even small things compared with the staggering heroism that many Americans show every day. In this nation, each day's newspaper brings stories of friends who donate their life savings to help a neighbor's child get an education, of relatives who donate kidneys or bone marrow, of men and women who shove small children out of the path of a truck and lose their own lives. There are many more such stories that never get into the newspapers. The solace that Mickey and I offered by sitting with bereaved friends was nothing at all unique. Certainly, Mickey and I claim no medals for what we have done.

But with all of that, there is—or so it seems to me—far less of everyday friendship and loyalty today than there was when I was growing up. You can see it in statistics— homeless people whose neighbors will not take them in, to the tune of three million as this book is written; children growing up in homes with only one parent, at least 25 percent of all small children today; an ever-rising number of Americans swindling other Americans and running off with their money. You can also see it on the street, in your neighborhood, out of your window.

As I look out at this golden America, I see the links between man and man simply dissolving. The ties of neighborhood, family, friends which were taken for granted twenty or thirty years ago are just memories for far too many Americans today. The late twentieth century model citizen of the United States of America is all too often an atom, separated from neighbors, from family, without friends, a tiny unit in the marketplace, and nothing more. A human being in this day has come to mean a production or consumption unit, and not a flesh-and-blood man or woman tied to the rest of the community, except by the wholly inadequate bonds of getting and spending.

Sometime after 1960, the mortar between the bricks of

the society started to dry up and blow away. I do not know whether it was because of inflation, or crime, or the war in Vietnam, or Watergate, or the collapse of education in much of America. Maybe the society just got too large for humans to feel much connection with each other. I know that in scientific experiments, when mice get crowded together, they stop acting cooperatively and start competing with each other and fighting with each other. Maybe that was what happened to human beings.

Or maybe in the drive to specialize and to maximize output, human beings stopped having the time to hear each other's problems. There is no butcher counter to hang around any longer and no butcher to chat with. In today's markets, the butchers are not even visible. They are in the back, being efficient. There are no soda fountains today (like the one I took Judy Turner to so long ago) because young people have part-time jobs and have to rush out and make money as soon as school is over each day, and soda fountains wouldn't make enough money to pay for the rent anyway. Today's store cannot have young people mooning over two Cokes. That is not a cost-efficient use of space.

Maybe nations go through phases, as people do, without our knowing the cause. Perhaps we as a nation have accomplished so much in the postwar period—growing, racial equality, advances in the emancipation of women, the high technologizing of America—that we are tired and irritable as a nation and need a period of calm to knit ourselves back together.

Frankly, I do not know for certain the reasons why the bonds of friendship and loyalty are so much more tenuous today than they were when I was younger. For whatever reason, men and women started to believe that they would be better off trying to make a dollar off their neighbor than helping their neighbor, that they would be ahead of the game if they rolled up their windows and just didn't hear other people crying out, that *the aim of life was not to have friends,* but to have *things,* that cunning was superior to loyalty, that getting ahead was better than keeping a friend.

As a judge, I saw and still see the results every day. Quarrels over silly things that should never last five minutes get into state courts. Neighbors who should be able to work out who gets a spare parking space have to get a judge to settle the matter. Daughters need a court to patch things up with their mothers. Children are alone. Men and women are alone. Older people are alone. We are become a nation of lonely people without the capacity to feel enough for others to work out the most basic disputes. More than that, we are becoming a nation of lonely people, two hundred and fifty million Americans living next door to each other without knowing each other's names.

I do not allow this to happen in my own life. As far as I can, I fight it in the lives of all that I love. Friendship and loyalty are my weapons in that fight.

I fight against the same lack of connection in court on television, just as I did on Superior Court in Los Angeles. Exactly as I tried to feel the pain of my friends when they lost their children, I tried and still try to feel the pain of the people who appear before me in litigation. It is my job, as I see it, to bring some feeling of connectedness (at least with me) into their lives. My responsibility is to let the men and women who appear before me know that the law is being interpreted and enforced by a human being who can feel their pain, who is part of their world. I try to be a judge and a neighbor as well to the people who come before me. If I could not act as a neighbor and a friend, I would not want the job. After all, the law is not inanimate software controlling robots. The law is the creature of people, its servant for the purpose of putting order and peace and justice into their lives. The law is, or should be, a neighbor itself, and a judge is no more than a particularly active part of the law.

But the law does not stand above or separate from what is happening in society generally. Not one judge nor one thousand judges can by themselves put back the glue into the relations between and among persons. Each man or woman will have to start doing that himself or herself if we are to again have a nation where people know who lives next door to them and care about them and are cared for in return.

I do not know precisely how people can start feeling for their neighbors again, start putting friendship and loyalty into the top ranks of human values once again. But I do know a good place to start. It's something we all know by heart, yet rarely give the attention it deserves:

Love thy neighbor as thyself

It's an ancient rule, but it still works.

FOR THE BEST IN PAPERBACKS, LOOK FOR THE 🐧

In every corner of the world, on every subject under the sun, Penguin represents quality and variety—the very best in publishing today.

For complete information about books available from Penguin—including Pelicans, Puffins, Peregrines, and Penguin Classics—and how to order them, write to us at the appropriate address below. Please note that for copyright reasons the selection of books varies from country to country.

In the United Kingdom: For a complete list of books available from Penguin in the U.K., please write to *Dept E.P., Penguin Books Ltd, Harmondsworth, Middlesex, UB7 0DA.*

In the United States: For a complete list of books available from Penguin in the U.S., please write to *Dept BA, Penguin, 299 Murray Hill Parkway, East Rutherford, New Jersey 07073.*

In Canada: For a complete list of books available from Penguin in Canada, please write to *Penguin Books Canada Ltd, 2801 John Street, Markham, Ontario L3R 1B4.*

In Australia: For a complete list of books available from Penguin in Australia, please write to the *Marketing Department, Penguin Books Australia Ltd, P.O. Box 257, Ringwood, Victoria 3134.*

In New Zealand: For a complete list of books available from Penguin in New Zealand, please write to the *Marketing Department, Penguin Books (NZ) Ltd, Private Bag, Takapuna, Auckland 9.*

In India: For a complete list of books available from Penguin, please write to *Penguin Overseas Ltd, 706 Eros Apartments, 56 Nehru Place, New Delhi, 110019.*

In Holland: For a complete list of books available from Penguin in Holland, please write to *Penguin Books Nederland B.V., Postbus 195, NL-1380AD Weesp, Netherlands.*

In Germany: For a complete list of books available from Penguin, please write to *Penguin Books Ltd, Friedrichstrasse 10-12, D-6000 Frankfurt Main 1, Federal Republic of Germany.*

In Spain: For a complete list of books available from Penguin in Spain, please write to *Longman Penguin España, Calle San Nicolas 15, E-28013 Madrid, Spain.*